OLD-FASHIONED
CROCHET

OLD-FASHIONED
CROCHET

EUNICE SVINICKI &
KARLA THOMPSON

VAN NOSTRAND REINHOLD COMPANY
New York Cincinnati Toronto London Melbourne

Copyright © 1981 by Van Nostrand Reinhold Company
Library of Congress Catalog Card Number 80-24742
ISBN 0-442-23120-2

Printed in the United States of America

Book Design by Jean Callan King/Visuality

Published by Van Nostrand Reinhold Company
135 West 50th Street, New York, N.Y. 10020

Van Nostrand Reinhold Limited
1410 Birchmount Road, Scarborough, Ontario M1P 2E7, Canada

Van Nostrand Reinhold Australia Pty. Limited
17 Queen Street, Mitcham, Victoria 3132, Australia

Van Nostrand Reinhold Company Limited
Molly Millars Lane, Wokingham, Berkshire, England

16 15 14 13 12 11 10 9 8 7 6 5 4 3 2 1

Library of Congress Cataloging in Publication Data
Svinicki, Eunice.
  Old-fashioned crochet.
  Bibliography: p.
  Includes index.
  1. Crocheting.   I. Thompson, Karla, joint author.
II. Title.
TT820.S94   746.43'4   80-24742
ISBN 0-442-23120-2

CONTENTS

INTRODUCTION

Crocheting has long been one of the most popular of needlecraft techniques. For decades crocheters have been catching threads with hooks to create beautiful combinations of stitches and pattern. Crochet can be simple or very fancy, depending upon the stitches used and the size of thread and hook, and for those who know and love crochet, filet, popcorn, pineapple, picot, and many of the other terms used in this book are already familiar.

With the resurgence of interest in the fine needlecrafts, old-fashioned crochet is reappearing. Once again, people are crocheting doilies, tablecloths, and bedspreads in the fine cotton threads. For some, this art was never lost, but only tucked away for a while. Hand-crocheted doilies and laces were popular up until some thirty years ago (when machine-made lace pieces took their place). Almost every home had a collection of hand-crocheted pieces placed under vases and lamps. Tablecloths were crocheted of fancy motifs or edged in a fancy crocheted cotton lace.

During the early part of this century, although crochet patterns were quite abundant, many women could not read or write. These women had to rely on their own resources to create original designs and to learn how to rework those crocheted articles they admired. Many simply took out their magnifying glasses to examine those admired pieces of crochet. By counting the various stitches, they were able to reproduce an exact or similar crocheted piece. One of the ways to keep patterns for future use was to make samples of laces and stitches so that they could easily be copied time after time. Many workbaskets not only held wonderful balls of thread and assorted hooks, but also a magnifying glass that enabled the crocheter to see every stitch clearly.

As the years went by, the fine steel hooks and cotton thread of fancy crochet gave way to bulky aluminum hooks and heavy colored yarns and the styles that go with them. Fortunately, the cotton threads are still made today, as are the fine steel hooks. They are readily available in most needlework departments or variety stores.

Poke around in the old trunk in the attic. Visit rummage sales and antique shops for old crochet work. Use the pieces as they are or use them as references for crocheting a new piece. In general, it is difficult to find written patterns, and it is for this reason that we have written *Old-Fashioned Crochet*. In it we have provided instructions for five techniques—motifs, filet crochet, Irish crochet, insertions, and trims—as well as numerous projects utilizing each of the techniques taught. We hope *Old-Fashioned Crochet* serves as a reminder and an inspiration to those of you who wish to revive and enjoy the fine art of old-fashioned crochet.

7

THE BASICS OF CROCHET

Crocheting is based on several simple stitches capable of endless variations. With the combination of hook, thread, and fingers, one can twist the thread into hundreds of different stitches and patterns. Crochet begins with a chain of stitches. The chain may be joined end to end into a ring to begin a motif, or it may be worked straight on for the length desired. From this base of chain stitches, the crochet hook pulls one loop of thread through another loop to continually build a pattern of stitches. The nature of the resulting pattern will depend upon which way the stitches are formed.

1-1. Detail of a portion of a bedspread crocheted in late 19th-century England. Quite possibly made as a gift for a missionary about to leave for foreign shores, the intricate filet pattern was worked in a thick white cotton. Reproduced with permission of Worthing Museum and Art Gallery, Worthing, Sussex, England.

1-2. An Irish crochet collar from the late 19th century. Reproduced with permission of National Museum of Ireland, Dublin, Ireland.

MATERIALS

Crochet hooks are used to pull new loops of thread through existing loops. Hooks are made out of steel, bone, or wood, and the sizes range for traditional work from a very fine number 14 to size 00. The hook should be shiny and sleek so that the thread will slip off easily. Since fancy crocheters do much finer work, steel crochet hooks are perhaps the best suited.

The crochet hook size should correspond to the size of the thread. If you are using an existing pattern, follow the designer's recommendations. If you are composing your own work, the following table should be of assistance.

Thread Number	Hook Number
10	00 – 5
20	6 – 9
30	9 – 11
40	11 – 12
50	12 – 14
70 – 150	14

THREADS

The old patterns were almost always worked in a fine cotton or linen thread, cotton being the more popular. The fine mercerized cottons are best for bringing out detail in the fancy crochet designs. You may wish to substitute some of the newer synthetic or new cotton threads which are easy to launder. In general, crochet thread is very resistant to washing and holds up well over the years.

The earliest cottons were available in balls of white or ecru. Today you can purchase practically any color. The crochet threads are highly twisted and strong. They are usually sold in balls, varying in yardage from sizes 10 on up to a very fine 150. The smaller the number of the

1-3. Hand-carved crochet hooks of sea wood and hardwood. Photographed by Jules Kliot.

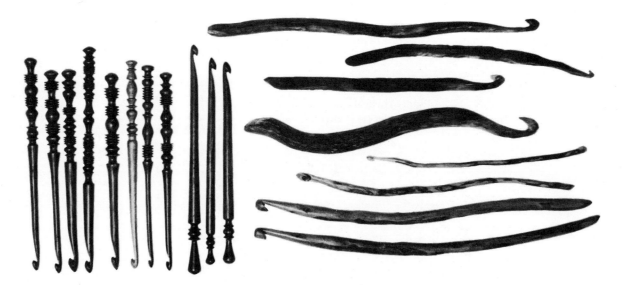

thread, the larger the thread is in thickness. Sometimes the heavier Knit-Cro-Sheen threads are put in skeins. Tatting thread may also be used for fancy crochet.

Regardless of which thread you buy remember to purchase sufficient quantities of one dye lot, even if it is white, so that you can finish the project without color variations.

STITCHES

Stitches are the basis of crochet. The patterns that result from your work will depend upon the stitches and stitch combinations you've used. Refer to the following directions.

Chain Stitch (ch)

A row of chain stitches is the first step of any crochet work, and the chain stitch is also used within patterns to create spaces. (See Abbreviations.)

Before you can make your row of chain stitches, you must first make a slip knot. Make a lp several inches from the thread end and hold between your thumb and forefinger. Pass hook through lp, under the thread, and catch the thread with the hook. Place thread over hook and pull thread through first lp (the slip knot) to make the first ch st. Rep pulling the lps through one another to make the desired number of ch sts. (See diagram.)

1-4. Chain Stitch.

1-5. Single Crochet.

Single Crochet (sc)

Single crochet is one of the shortest of all crochet stitches. When it is worked row after row, it will create a tight uniform stitch without spaces. (See Abbreviations.)

STEP 1: Make a ch of the desired length. Insert hook into 2nd ch st from hook. Place thread over hook. (See diagram.)

1-6. Single Crochet—Step 1.

STEP 2: Pull thread through lps to make 2 lps on the hook.

11

STEP 3: Place thread over hook again. (See diagram.)

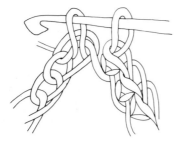

1-7. Single Crochet—Step 3.

STEP 4: Pull the thread through the 2 lps on the hook to make 1 lp. This completes 1 sc. (See diagram.)

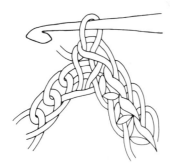

1-8. Single Crochet—Step 4.

STEP 5: To continue across the ch, insert hook into next ch st; rep.

NOTE: The hook may be inserted into the stitch through both loops or through either front or back loop of stitch. The way the hook is inserted produces different results. If you desire a ridge effect throughout the piece, insert the hook through one loop only. This also produces a slightly loose stitch. Note, however, that this should be done consistently throughout the work. The other alternative is to insert the hook through both loops, which will result in work that is flat and smooth. Be sure to check your instructions to see if there are specific directions.

1-9. Double Crochet.

Double Crochet (dc)

The double crochet is probably the most used of all crochet stitches. It is taller than the single crochet but yet produces firm work. (See Abbreviations.)

STEP 1: Make a ch of the desired length. With thread over hook, insert hook into 4th ch st from the hook.

STEP 2: Place thread over hook again.

1-10. Double Crochet—Steps 1 to 3.

STEP 3: Pull thread through. There should be 3 lps on the hook. (See diagram.)
STEP 4: Place thread over hook.
STEP 5: Pull thread over 2 lps. There should be 2 lps on the hook now.
STEP 6: Place thread over hook. (See diagram.)

1-13. Half Double Crochet.

·1-11. Double Crochet—Steps 4 to 6.

STEP 7: Pull thread through the 2 lps on hook. One dc is now complete. (See diagram.)

body and sturdiness. It is a tighter stitch and resembles knitting. (See Abbreviations.)
STEP 1: Make a ch of the desired length, place thread over hook, and insert hook into 3rd ch st from hook.
STEP 2: Place thread over hook again.
STEP 3: Pull thread through ch. There are now 3 lps on the hook. (See diagram.)

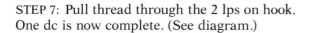

1-12. Double Crochet—Step 7.

STEP 8: To continue across the ch, place thread over hook, insert hook into the next ch and rep Steps 2 to 7.

Half Double Crochet (hdc)

Next to single crochet, this stitch is the easiest to execute. It is used where the crocheter wants

1-14. Half Double Crochet—Steps 1 to 3.

STEP 4: Place thread over hook.
STEP 5: Pull thread over 3 lps on hook. One hdc is now complete. (See diagram.)

1-15. Half Double Crochet—Steps 4 to 5.

STEP 6: To continue across, place thread over hook and insert hook into next ch and rep Steps 2 to 5.

Treble (Triple) Crochet (tr)

This stitch is not used as often as the others because it is very loose. It works very well,

1-16. Treble Crochet.

1-17. Treble Crochet in progress.

however, when a lacy look is needed. (See Abbreviations.)
STEP 1: Make a ch of the desired length. Place thread over hook twice and insert hook into 5th ch st from hook.
STEP 2: Place thread over hook. (See diagram.)
STEP 3: Pull thread through 1 lp. There are now 4 lps on hook.
STEP 4: Place thread over hook.
STEP 5: Pull thread through 2 lps on hook (3 lps left on hook).
STEP 6: Place thread over hook.
STEP 7: Pull thread through 2 lps on hook, place thread over hook, and pull through last 2 lps. One tr is now complete.
STEP 8: To continue across, place thread twice over hook and insert into next ch st. Rep Steps 2 to 7.

Slip Stitch: (sl st)

A slip stitch is used basically as a finishing stitch. It gives your work a smooth edge. It is also used as a means of working over to another stitch without adding height to a design. (See Abbreviations.)
STEP 1: Make a ch of the desired length.

14

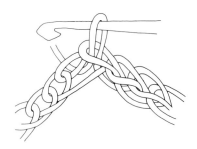

1-18. Slip Stitch.

STEP 2: Place thread over hook and insert into 2nd ch from hook.
STEP 3: Yo hook and draw a lp through both the ch and lp on hook. One sl st is now complete. (See diagram.)

Decreasing Stitches

The method you should use to decrease stitches will depend on the stitch with which you are working.

In single crochet: Insert hook into st, place thread over hook and pull through 1 lp. Insert hook into next st, place thread over hook, and pull thread through 1 lp. Place thread over hook and pull through 3 lps on hook.

In double crochet: Place thread over hook, insert hook into next st, place thread over hook, and pull through 1 lp. Place thread over hook and pull through 2 lps (2 lps left on hook). Place thread over hook. Insert hook into next st, place thread over hook, and pull through 1 lp. Place thread over hook and pull through 2 lps. Place thread over hook and draw through 3 remaining lps on hook.

An alternate method of decreasing is to simply skip over *one* stitch at a time, usually at the beginning or the end of a row. This is not a hard and fast rule however. The eye must dictate where decreases will look best.

Increasing Stitches

Make an increase by working two stitches of any kind into one stitch.

FORMING A ROUND

First start out by working a ring. To do this make a chain of the desired length, insert hook into first chain, and join with a slip stitch. Next, work the stitches into and around the ring. Join the last stitch to the first with a slip stitch. Work the next round into the stitches made by the first round. A spiral is made by not joining each round together with a slip stitch.

TURNING WORK

A certain number of chain stitches must be made at the end of each row so that the work can be placed in position again for the next row. The number of chains will depend upon the length of the stitch worked in the row. Here are some guidelines:

Stitch: Directions for Turning

SINGLE CROCHET: Ch 1, work in 2nd ch from hook
HALF DOUBLE CROCHET: Ch 2, work in 3rd ch from hook
DOUBLE CROCHET: Ch 3, work in 4th ch from hook

15

TREBLE CROCHET: Ch 4, work in 5th ch from hook

After the chains have been worked, the piece is turned around and the next row worked.

ENDING WORK

To end work, do not work the turning chain stitches at the end of the last row. Instead, cut thread several inches from work and bring end through final loop on hook. Weave the end back into the work.

PATTERN STITCHES

Pattern stitches are the result of combining basic stitches. The combinations are endless. Listed below are a few of the more common ones.

Shell Stitch

The shell is worked in groups of three or more stitches worked into one stitch. The photograph shows a basic shell pattern, but there are many variations possible. A shell stitch usually consists of a variety of stitches with the tallest one in the middle to create a fan effect. Here are the basic directions (see Abbreviations).

ROW 1: Make 2 dc in 4th ch from hook, * sk 2 chs, sc in next ch, sk 2 chs, 5 dc in next ch, rep from * across row, end with sk 2 chs, sc in last ch, ch 3, turn.

ROW 2: Make 2 dc in first sc of previous row * sc in center dc st of shell, 5 dc in next sc, rep from * across row, end with 1 sc in top of turning ch, ch 3, turn.

Rep Row 2 for pat.

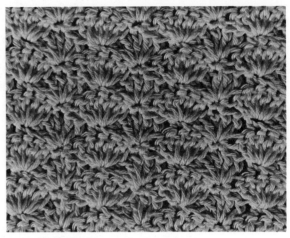

1-19. Shell Stitch.

1-20. Cluster Stitch.

Cluster Stitch

The cluster stitch is made of two or more stitches gathered together. A multiple of three stitches plus one is needed to work the pattern. Below is a basic cluster pattern. (See Abbreviations.) However, the possibilities are endless when it comes to cluster combinations.

16

ROW 1: Insert hook into 4th ch from hook, (yo, pull through a lp, yo and through 2 lps) twice; yo and through the 3 lps on hook, * ch 2, sk 2 chs, (yo, insert hook in next ch, yo, pull through 1 lp, yo and through 2 lps) 3 times; yo and through 4 lps on hook [1 cluster made.] Rep from * across row, end with ch 3, turn.

ROW 2: (Yo, insert hook in top of cluster of first row, pull through a lp, yo and through 2 lps) twice; yo and through the 3 lps on hook, ch 2, make a cluster in next cluster of first row. Rep from * across, end with ch 3, turn.

Rep Row 2 for pat.

Puff Stitch

The puff stitch is a variation of the cluster stitch. A multiple of four stitches is needed to repeat the puff stitch. Follow these directions (see Abbreviations).

ROW 1: Insert hook into 2nd chain from hook, sc in first 3 sts, *yo, insert hook into next st, yo, pull through 1 lp, (yo, insert into same st, yo, pull through 1 lp) twice; yo and pull through the 7 lps on hook. Sc in each of next 3 sts. Rep from * across, ch 1, turn.

ROW 2: Sc in each st across, end with ch 1, turn.

Rep Rows 1 and 2 for pat.

Popcorn Stitch

This stitch gathers into a higher, more rounded puff. A multiple of four plus two stitches is needed. Follow these directions (see Abbreviations).

ROW 1: Dc in 4th st from hook, dc in next 2 sts, * 5 dc in top of next st; remove hook and insert hook into back of first dc of the grouping of 5 dc, insert hook into dropped lp and pull it through lp on hook; dc in each of next 3 dc. Rep from * across, ch 3, turn.

ROW 2: Starting in 4th chain from hook, sc in each st across, ch 3, turn.

Rep Rows 1 and 2 for pat.

1-21. Puff Stitch.

1-22. Popcorn Stitch.

GAUGE

The gauge is measured by the number of stitches and rows per inch. To check the gauge, place a tape measure on a row and count the number of stitches per inch. Place the tape measure vertically and count the number of rows per inch. If you are following a pattern which gives a particular gauge, your gauge should be adjusted to meet the gauge in the instructions. If your measure is smaller than the gauge, change to a larger hook, or, for example, if the gauge lists four stitches per inch and you come up with a larger number of stitches per inch, then you are crocheting too tight and should have a larger hook.

Some crocheters work very tightly or very loosely. If you are one of the above, it is a good idea to do a sample swatch in order to guarantee gauge.

CHANGING COLORS OR ATTACHING ANOTHER BALL OF THREAD

Your aim in changing colors or attaching new thread is to do so without leaving a bulge. This might take some practice.

Insert hook into work and work the thread

1-23. Changing colors or attaching another ball of thread.

over with the next color thread. Cut off the first color and leave a 1- to 2-inch end of the second color. After work is completed, weave in loose ends. (See diagram.) If you are just changing colors over a small area, twist the first color around the second, and carry it loosely across the back until you pick it up again.

CLEANING AND BLOCKING

Crocheted pieces are marvelously strong constructions. It is not uncommon to find an old piece of crochet-trimmed fabric on which the fabric portion has long since rotted away and the crochet portion is still very much intact. Old cotton crochet can be cleaned in a mild, lukewarm solution of soap and water. A special detergent called Orvus Paste (Proctor and Gamble) may also be used. Swish the piece through the sudsy water. Squeeze out the excess water, but do not wring. Rinse thoroughly until the water is clear and squeeze out the excess water again. Lay the piece on a turkish towel and stretch it into the correct size and shape. Allow it to air-dry this way. Place rust-proof pins close together. Some fancy items may need pinning to shape. Press the crocheted pieces after they have dried.

If you are blocking an extremely fancy piece of crochet, it is necessary to pin at each point. It is also a good idea to press your work slightly, even if it has been blocked in this way. This makes it lie flat. Other pieces of work that are less complicated or flat can be simply pressed with a steam iron.

Stains may be removed in a solution of sodium perborate which can be purchased at the drugstore. Use one tablespoon to two quarts of lukewarm water.

Rust stains can be removed in a solution of oxalic acid, also available at drugstores. Use one-half tablespoon to one-half cup water and then spot treat the stain. Rinse the fabric thoroughly after the stain is gone.

FINISHING

If you want a stiffer finish, starch the work after it is crocheted. Laundry starch works well for most pieces. The glossy laundry starch which must be cooked works best for heavier finishes. Follow the manufacturer's directions for the degree of stiffness desired. For light finishing, instant laundry starch will work equally well. Years ago, many households used sugar as a stiffening agent. For crocheted pieces, such as baskets, which require a great deal of stiffness, sugar works very well.

READING PATTERNS

Most crochet pattern instructions are a language of abbreviations. Since pattern instructions almost always include abbreviations, it is wise to refer to the following list when reading the pattern directions.

Abbreviations

beg: beginning
ch: chain stitch
dc: double crochet
dec: decrease
hdc: half double crochet
inc: increase
lp(s): loop(s)
pat(s): pattern(s)
rep: repeat
rnd(s): round(s)
sc: single crochet
sk: skip
sl st: slip stitch
sp: space
st(s): stitch(es)
tog: together
tr: treble or triple crochet
yo: yarn over hook
* repeat directions from * as many times as indicated
( ): repeat
    For example (sc, ch 2), 3 times means work stitches within the parentheses 3 times.
multiple of: used to indicate how many stitches are needed to work the pattern.
    For example, a multiple of 5 stitches means that 5, 10, 15, 20, and so on is the number of stitches needed to complete the pattern stitch. In such a multiple, 8 or 13 stitches, for example, would not give a complete pattern.

C H A P T E R T W O

MOTIFS

A motif is a combination of stitches worked in symmetrical fashion. Popcorns, clusters, double crochets, ridges, and chains are just some of the stitches which might be found in a motif. Beginning from a central point, the stitches of a motif are worked round and round from the center. Motifs can be worked in any symmetrical fashion—a square, circle, a hexagon. Alone, a motif stands as a doily, such as the one in Figure 2-1, a cover for a small pillow, or a pincushion. Assembled together, motifs can become bedspreads, afghans, and tablecloths. Crocheters of the early part of this century manipulated their hooks and threads into very fancy and delicate pieces. Today, you can do the same.

Following are directions for working a few basic motifs. If you are an accomplished crocheter, you should have no difficulty creating your own motifs. Refer to the books listed in the Bibliography for additional motif patterns, and see Figures 2-1 through 2-12 for fine examples.

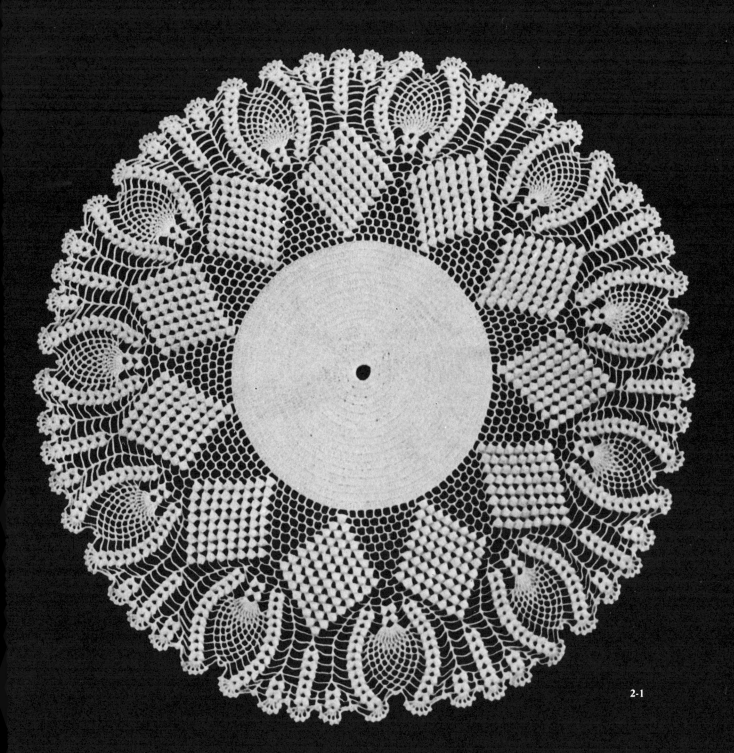

2-1

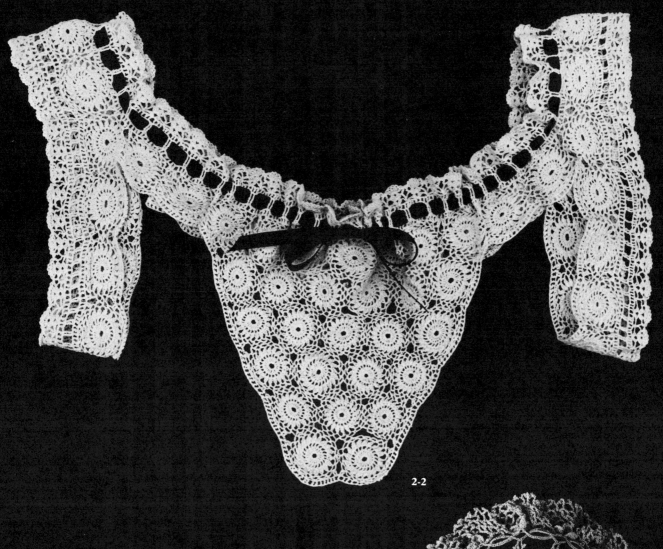

2-2

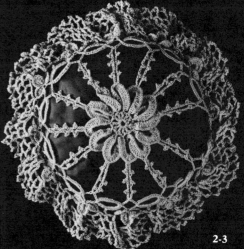

2-3

22

2-4

2-5

23

2-6

24

2-7

2-8

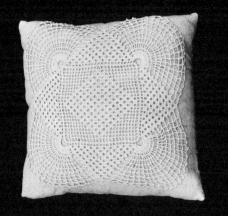

2-9

2-10

2-11

2-12

2-1. A contemporary doily with popcorn stitches and pineapple motifs recreated by Victoria Dougovito from an antique.

2-2. An antique camisole top made of small motifs with a ribbon insertion. From a collection of Eunice Svinicki.

2-3. An antique pincushion made of burgundy-colored satin and ecru cotton thread. From the collection of Tinder Box Antiques.

2-4. A pinwheel doily. From the collection of Karla Thompson.

2-5. A doily made of nine fancy motifs. From the collection of Karla Thompson.

2-6. A fancy dresser scarf. From the collection of Helene Svinicki.

2-7. A traditional pineapple motif doily. Made by Tina Bergman. Tina Bergman was a prolific crocheter, who made hundreds of beautiful designs during her 92 years of life, several of which appear in this book.

2-8. A popcorn motif doily made by Victoria Dougovito.

2-9. A doily motif used as a pillow top. From the collection of Eunice Svinicki.

2-10. A round motif used as a top for a pincushion. From the collection of Harriet Koller.

2-11. Detail of a pinwheel motif doily. From the collection of Eunice Svinicki.

2-12. A doily for which motifs were whipstitched together, made by Tina Bergman.

BASIC MOTIF SHAPES

Following are the directions for the basic shapes of motifs. If you are an experimenter in design, use these directions to create any basic symmetrical shape you want. Substitute any stitch combination to make your motif fancy.

Circle

To make a circular crocheted piece you must work in rounds, increasing stitches in regular sequence in such a way that the work will lie flat. Too many increases will cause a circle to ruffle; too few will make it pucker.

There are two approaches to making a circle. One is to join each round of crochet stitches with a slip stitch. The other is to not join each round with a slip stitch, but to just keep crocheting around. This creates a spiral of stitches, and there won't be a seam line. If you choose to work this way, be sure to mark the first stitch of each round with a safety pin so that you will be able to keep track of rounds and, therefore, increase accordingly. Regardless of which method you use, increasing properly is a most important part of building good circle motifs.

The following example of a joined circle is worked in single crochet, but you can substitute double crochet, half double crochet, or treble crochet, if you wish. Just be sure to make the appropriate adjustment when chaining up. (See Note under Round 1.)

TO START: Ch 6, join with sl st.

RND 1: Ch 1 [*Note:* Ch as many as is necessary to equal the st you are working in; i.e., ch 1 = sc, ch 2 = dc or hdc, ch 3 = tr], make 11 sc in ring, join with sl st to first sc.

RND 2: Ch 1, 2 sc in each sc around. End with sl st to first ch 1.

RND 3 AND SUBSEQUENT RNDS: From here on make 2 sc in each st of the previous rnd, and inc sts in regular intervals in such a way that the work will lie flat.

Square

Square motifs are also worked in rounds. To make a square motif you will start out with a ring of stitches and then you will work a three-stitch increase at each of four points to create the corners of the square.

Work squares with a multiple of four stitches into the ring. This multiple of four stitches is used throughout the shaping. You then divide the number of stitches used by four to determine the number of stitches to make for each side of the square in the first round. For example, if you have twelve stitches worked into the ring, that would allow three stitches for each side of the first round of the square. Work one-quarter of the total number of stitches (in this case, three), then work three stitches for a corner. Repeat for the other three sides. Join with a slip stitch to the beginning stitch. Continue increasing evenly around and working the same number of stitches on each side. Work three stitches in each corner.

The following example is worked in dc, but you can substitute single crochet, half double crochet, or treble crochet, if you wish. See Note under Round 1 of Circle.

TO START: Ch 6, join with a sl st.

RND 1: Ch 3, make 11 dc in ring, end with sl st to top of ch 3 [12 dc in ring].

RND 2: Ch 3, 1 dc in next 2 dc, *ch 3 1 dc in next 3 dc, rep from * around until there are 4 groups of 3 dc completed. End with ch 3, sl st to top of first ch 3.

RND 3: Ch 3, 1 dc in next 2 dc, (3 dc in ch-3 sp, ch 3, 3 dc in same ch-3 sp), 1 dc in next 3 dc. Rep from * around, end with sl st to first ch 3.

RND 4: Ch 3, 1 dc in next 5 dc, 3 dc in ch-3 sp, ch 3, 3 dc in same ch-3 sp, * 1 dc in next 9 dc, (3 dc in ch-3 sp, ch 3, 3 dc in same ch-3 sp). Rep from * around. Finish rnd with 1 dc in last 3 dc, end with sl st to top of ch 3.

RND 5 AND SUBSEQUENT RNDS: Rep Rnd 4. Remember there will be added dcs per side as the piece of work progresses.

Hexagon

A hexagon is worked in much the same manner as a square, except, of course, there are six sides and you must, therefore, start with a multiple of six stitches. Divide the work into sixths and increase three stitches in every corner one-sixth of the way around. Work evenly around, increasing three stitches in each corner. Join with a slip stitch to the first stitch.

The following example is done in double crochet, but you can substitute single crochet, half double crochet, or treble crochet, if you wish. See the Note under Round 1 of Circle.

TO START: Ch 6, join with a sl st.

RND 1: Ch 3, make 17 dc in ring, join with a sl st to top of ch 3.

RND 2: Ch 3, make 1 dc in next 2 dc * ch 3, 1 dc in next 3 dc, rep from * around, end with ch 3, sl st to top of first ch 3.

RND 3: Ch 3, 1 dc in next 2 dc, *(1 dc in ch-3 sp, ch 3, 1 dc in same ch-3 sp), 1 dc in next 3 dc. Rep from * around, end with ch 3, 1 dc in ch-3 sp. Sl st to top of first ch 3.

RND 4 AND SUBSEQUENT RNDS: Rep Rnd 3. Remember there will be added sts per side as the work progresses.

Octagon

An octagon is worked in the same manner as a hexagon, except you will be starting with a multiple of eight stitches. Then you will divide the work into eighths and increase three stitches in every corner one-eighth of the way around.

The following example is done in double crochet, but you can substitute single crochet, half double crochet, or treble crochet, if you wish. See the Note under Round 1 of Circle.

TO START: Ch 6, join with a sl st.

RND 1: Ch 3, make 23 dc in ring. Join with sl st to top of ch 3.

RND 2: Ch 3, 1 dc in next 2 dc, ch 3, * 1 dc in next 3 dc. Rep from * around, end with ch 3, sl st to top of ch 3 [8 groups of 3 dc with ch 3 between them].

RND 3: Ch 3, 1 dc in next 2 dc, *(1 dc in ch-3 sp, ch 3, 1 dc in same ch-3 sp), 1 dc in next 3 dc. Rep from * around, end with ch 3, 1 dc in ch-3 sp. Attach with sl st to top of ch 3.

RND 4 AND SUBSEQUENT RNDS: Remember there will be added sts per side as the work progresses.

Oval

An oval motif is made in a different manner. The first step is to decide upon a size for the finished motif. Your starting chain must be equal in length to the difference between the length and width of the desired motif. (For example, if the motif is to be 6 by 8 inches, you would start out with a 2-inch chain.) You will then work one stitch in each chain across, and three stitches in the last chain of the row. Without turning, you then work the bottom edge of the chain, continuing around until you complete the chain. Join with a slip stitch to the first chain and continue around as you would for a circle, increasing three stitches at each end. You may need to increase more stitches as the size increases.

 Work this example:

TO START: Make a ch 2 inches long. Work 11 dc in each ch up to last ch. In last ch work 4 dc. [You will perhaps find it necessary to either inc to 5 dc or dec to 3 dc. The decision must be made if the oval is puckering.] Do not turn work.

RND 1: Make 1 dc in each st of bottom edge. In last st work 4 dc.

RND 2: There is no need to sl st each rnd. Continue rnd by rnd as before.

JOINING MOTIFS

If you are just making a single motif, there is no other work required. But, if you are planning to assemble several motifs to make an afghan or tablecloth, for example, you will have to learn how to join them together artfully. There are several ways to join motifs, and the shape and design of the particular motif will largely determine how they should be joined.

Joining After Crocheting

Following are three methods, each of which can be used to join motifs with long, straight edges, such as triangles and squares. The joining is done after all of the motifs to be assembled have been crocheted.

Method 1:
This first method creates a seamed appearance. Place motifs right sides together. Sew them together with overcast stitches, making a narrow seam. (See diagram.) This method creates a definite joining line and a right and wrong side.

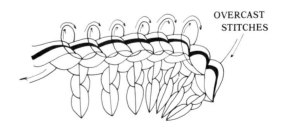

OVERCAST STITCHES

2-13. Joining after motifs are crocheted—Method 1.

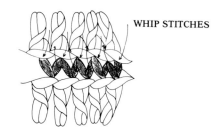

WHIP STITCHES

2-14. Joining after motifs are crocheted— Method 2.

Method 2:
This method creates a flatter piece without a raised joining line. Place motifs side by side, right sides up, and whip-stitch the edges together. For each stitch, catch the back loop of one stitch from each motif.

Method 3:
This method creates a raised ridge on the right side of the piece. Place motifs wrong sides together. Single crochet or slip-stitch the edges together.

THREAD TO ATTACH MOTIFS

EDGE OF MOTIF

2-15. Joining after motifs are crocheted— Method 3.

Joining While Crocheting

Motifs may also be joined together while the crocheting is in progress. This is a common way to join circles and ovals.

Complete the first motif and the second motif up to the last round. Join the second to the first motif at points where they meet on adjacent sides. You may also use a whip stitch to join motifs. Catch the back thread of one stitch

30

from each motif. Usually project directions will specify how to join circle or oval motifs.

Filling In Spaces

Some motifs are lacy and have many different points that leave a space after assemblage. Another smaller motif is crocheted as a filler between the dominant motifs. The points of each motif are sewn together using an overcast stitch.

GEOMETRIC HEXAGON MOTIF

Size

5 inches in diameter

Thread

1 ball (200 yards) mercerized crochet cotton, number 10

Hook

size 7

Directions

TO START: Ch 10, sl st to first ch to form ring.
RND 1: Ch 3, 3 dc in ring, * ch 1, 4 dc in ring, rep from * until 6 groups of 4 dc are complete. End with ch 1, sl st to top of first ch 3.
RND 2: Ch 3, 1 dc in same place as sl st; 1 dc in each of next 3 dc, 1 dc in ch-1 sp [6 dc]; * ch 1, 1 dc in same ch-1 sp and in each of next 4 dc, 1 dc in ch-1 sp; rep from * around. End with ch 1, sl st to top of first ch 3.
RNDS 3–7: Work as for previous rnd except inc 1 dc at beg and 1 dc at end of each side.
RNDS 8–10: 1 hdc in each dc around. Inc as in Rnds 3–7.
NOTE: Always ch 1 between last 1-dc inc and first 1-dc inc for each section.

RND 11: * (Ch 4, sk 1 hdc, 1 sc in next hdc), rep between ( ) 10 times; 3 sc in corner sp. Rep from * around. End with sl st to top of first ch 4. Fasten off.

POPCORN MOTIF

Size

4½ by 4½ inches

Thread

1 ball (200 yards) mercerized crochet cotton, number 10

Hook

size 7

Directions

TO START: Ch 6, sl st to first ch to form ring.
RND 1: Ch 3, 2 dc in ring, * ch 2, 3 dc in ring, rep from * until 4 groups of 3 dc are completed. End with ch 2, sl st to top of first ch 3 to join. Turn work.
RND 2: Ch 3, * make 1 popcorn st (see Note) in ch-2 sp, ch 2, make another popcorn st in same ch-2 sp, ch 2, rep from * around. End with sl st to top of first ch 3 to join. Sl st up to first ch-2 sp.
NOTE: See page 17 for directions on popcorn st. The first ch 3 of rnds using the popcorn st is included as part of first popcorn st only.
RND 3: Ch 3, 1 popcorn st in first ch-2 sp, ch 2, 1 popcorn st in same ch-2 sp, * ch 2, 1 popcorn st in next ch-2 sp, ch 2, ** 1 popcorn st in next ch-2 sp, ch 2, 1 popcorn st in same ch-2 sp, [corner], rep from * 3 times. Rep from * to ** 1 time. End with ch 2, sl st to top of first ch 3 to join. Sl st up to first ch-2 sp.

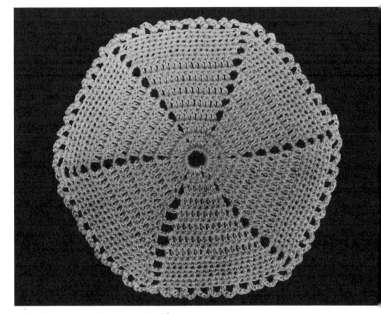

2-16. Geometric Hexagon Motif.

2-17. Popcorn Motif.

31

RND 4: Ch 4, 2 tr in first ch-2 corner sp, ch 2, 3 tr in same ch-2 corner sp, * (ch 2, 3 tr in next ch-2 sp), rep between ( ) 2 times; ch 2, ** 3 tr in ch-2 corner sp, ch 2, 3 tr in same ch-2 corner sp, rep from * 3 times. Rep from * to ** 1 time. End with sl st to top of first ch 4 to join. Sl st up to ch-2 corner sp.

RND 5: Ch 2, 1 hdc in first ch-2 corner sp, ch 2, 2 hdc in same ch-2 corner sp; * (1 hdc in each of tr and each ch-2 sp) across to next corner; ** work corner with 2 hdc in ch-2 corner sp, ch 2, 2 hdc in same ch-2 corner sp; rep from * 3 times. Rep from * to ** 1 time. End with sl st to top of first ch 2 to join. Sl st up to ch-2 corner sp.

RND 6: Ch 3, 1 popcorn st in ch-2 corner sp, ch 2, 1 popcorn st in same ch-2 corner sp, * ch 2, 1 hdc in each hdc across to next corner, ch 2, **, 1 popcorn st in ch-2 corner sp, ch 2, 1 popcorn st in same ch-2 corner sp; rep from * 3 times. Rep from * to ** 1 time. End with sl st to first popcorn st.

RND 7: Ch 3, 1 popcorn st in ch-2 corner sp, ch 2, 1 popcorn st in same ch-2 corner sp, * ch 2, 1 sc in next ch-2 sp, (ch 4, sk 2 hdc, 1 sc in next hdc), rep between ( ) 5 times; ch 4, sk 2 hdc, 1 sc in ch-2 sp, ch 2; ** 1 popcorn st in ch-2 corner sp, ch 2, 1 popcorn st in same ch-2 sp, rep from * 3 times. Rep from * to ** 1 time. End with sl st to first popcorn st to join.

RND 8: Ch 3, * 1 popcorn st in ch-2 corner sp, ch 2, 1 popcorn st in same ch-2 sp, 1 sc in ch-2 sp, (ch 4, 1 sc in next ch-4 sp), rep between ( ) 6 times; ch 4, 1 sc in ch-2 sp, ch 2, ** 1 popcorn st in ch-2 corner sp, ch 2, 1 popcorn st in same ch-2 corner sp; rep from * 3 times. Rep from * to ** once. End with sl st to first popcorn st to join.

RND 9: Ch 3, 2 dc in ch-2 corner sp, ch 2, 3 dc in same ch-2 corner sp, * ch 2, 1 sc in next ch-2 sp, (ch 4, 1 sc in next ch-4 sp), rep between ( ) 7 times; ch 4, 1 sc in ch-2 sp, ch 2; ** 3 dc in ch-2 corner sp, ch 2, 3 dc in same ch-2 corner sp; rep from * 3 times. Rep from * to ** once. End with sl st to top of first ch 3 to join. Sl st up to first ch-2 sp.

RND 10: Rep Rnd 9, repeating directions between ( ) 8 times.

RND 11: Rep Rnd 9, repeating directions between ( ) 9 times.

TO MAKE BORDER: Ch 3, 2 dc in ch-2 corner sp, ch 2, 3 dc in same ch-2 corner sp, * hdc in ch-2 sp, 4 hdc in each of ch-4 sps across to next corner with 2 hdc in ch-2 sp next to corner; 3 dc in ch-2 corner sp, ch 2, 3 dc in ch-2 corner sp. Rep from * around, end with sl st to top of first ch 3 to join. Fasten off.

GEOMETRIC PENTAGON MOTIF

Size
5 by 5 inches

Thread
1 ball (200 yards) mercerized crochet cotton, number 10

Hook
size 7

Directions

TO START: Ch 6, sl st to first ch to form ring.

RND 1: Ch 3, work 2 dc in ring, * ch 2, 3 dc in ring; rep from * until 5 groups of 3 dc are completed. End with ch 2, sl st to top of first ch 3 to join.

RND 2: Ch 3, turn. Work (2 dc, ch 2, 3 dc) in ch-3 sp to form shell. * Ch 1, work (3 dc, ch 2, 3 dc) in next ch-2 sp to form another shell. Rep from * until 5 shells are completed. End with ch 1, sl st up to top of first ch 3.

RND 3: Ch 3, turn. Work 2 dc in first ch-2 sp; *(ch 1, 3 dc, ch 2, 3 dc) in ch-2 corner sp to form corner shell; ch 1, 3 dc in next ch-1 sp. Rep from * around. End with ch 1, sl st to top of first ch 3.

RND 4: Continue as for previous rnd except add an additional group of 3 dc on each side.

RND 5: Ch 2, * work 1 hdc in each dc and 1 hdc in each ch-1 sp across to corner sp; (1 hdc, ch 1, 1 hdc) in ch-2 corner sp; rep from * around. End with sl st to first ch 2.

RND 6: Ch 2, * work 1 hdc in each st across to corner sp, (1 hdc, ch 1, 1 hdc) in ch-1 corner sp, rep from * around. End with sl st to first ch 2.

RND 7: Work as for previous rnds except ch 2 at corners.

RND 8: Work as for previous rnds except work 2 hdc in corner sp.

RND 9: Ch 3, 1 dc in each of next 2 hdc, ch 2, *sk 1 hdc, 1 dc in each of next 3 hdc, rep from * around, working corners as follows: Between 2 hdc of previous rnd, work 3 dc, ch 2, 3 dc. End with ch 2, sl st to top of first ch 3.

RND 10: Continue with shell pat as for Rnd 9, except ch 1 between 3 dcs. Corners are worked the same as Rnd 9. End with sl st to join. Fasten off.

FANCY MOTIF

Size

4 by 4 inches

Thread

1 ball (200 yards) mercerized crochet cotton, number 10

Hook

size 7

2-18. Geometric Pentagon Motif.

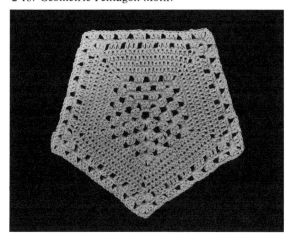

2-19. Fancy Motif.

Directions

TO START: Ch 8, sl st to first ch to form ring.

RND 1: Work first cluster as follows: Ch 3, (yo hook twice, insert hook into ring, yo hook, pull lp through, yo hook, pull lp through 2 lps, yo hook, pull lp through 2 lps) rep between ( ) 2 times; yo hook; pull through all lps on hook [1 cluster st made]. Work remaining clusters as follows: *Ch 2 (yo hook twice, insert hook into ring, pull lp through, yo hook, pull lp through 2 lps, yo hook, pull lp through 2 lps), rep between ( ) 3 times, pull through all lps on hook [1 cluster made]; rep from * until 8 clusters have been made. End with ch 2, sl st to top of first ch 3 to join.

RND 2: Sl st up to first ch-2 sp, ch 3, 3 tr in same ch-2 sp, *ch 3, 4 tr in next ch-2, rep from * until 8 4-trs are completed. End with ch 3, sl st to top of first ch 3 to join.

RND 3: Ch 3, 1 dc in next tr, ch 3, 1 dc in each of next 2 tr [corner]; *ch 2, 1 sc in next ch-3 sp, ch 2, 1 dc in each of next 4 tr, ch 2, 1 sc in next ch-3 sp, ch 2; **1 dc in each of next 2 tr, ch 3, 1 dc in each of next 2 tr [corner], rep from * 3 times. Rep from * to ** 1 more time. End with sl st to top of first ch 3 to join.

RND 4: Sl st up to ch-3 sp, ch 3, 3 tr in ch-3 corner sp, ch 3, 4 tr in same ch-3 corner sp, *ch 2, 1 sc in sc, ch 2, 1 tr in each of next 4 dc, ch 2, 1 sc in sc, ch 2 ** 4 tr in next ch-3 corner sp, ch 3, 4 tr in same ch-3 sp, rep from * 3 times. Rep from * to ** 1 time. End with sl st to top of first ch 3 to join.

RND 5: Sl st up to 3-ch sp, ch 4, 1 sc in same ch-3 corner sp, *(ch 5, 1 sc in next ch-2 sp), rep between ( ) 4 times; ch 5, **1 sc in ch-3 corner sp, ch 4, 1 sc in same ch-3 corner sp; rep from * 3 times. Rep from * to ** 1 time. End with sl st to base of ch 4 to join.

RND 6: Make 4 sl st in next ch-4 sp; ch 4, 3 tr in same ch-4 sp, ch 2, 4 tr in same ch-4 sp; *(ch 2, 1 sc in ch-5 sp, ch 2, 3 dc in next ch-5 sp), rep between ( ) 2 times; ch 2, 1 sc in next ch-5 sp, ch 2; ** 4 tr in ch-4 corner sp, ch 2, 4 tr in same ch-4 corner sp; rep from * 3 times. Rep from * to ** 1 time. End with sl st to top of first ch 4 to join.

RND 7: Sl st up to ch-2 corner sp, ch 4, 1 sc in same ch-2 sp, *(ch 5, 1 sc in next ch 2 sp), rep between ( ) 6 times; ch 5, **, 1 sc in ch-2 corner sp, ch 4, 1 sc in same ch-2 corner sp; rep from * 3 times. Rep from * to ** 1 time. End sl st to base of first ch 4 to join.

RND 8: Ch 4, 1 sc in ch-4 corner sp, *(ch 5, 1 sc in next ch-5 sp), rep between ( ) 7 times; ch 5, ** 1 sc in ch-4 corner sp, ch 4, 1 sc in same ch-4 corner sp, rep from * 3 times. Rep from * to ** 1 time. End with sl st to base of first ch 4 to join. Fasten off.

RAINDROP MOTIF

Size

4½ by 4½ inches

Thread

1 ball (200 yards) mercerized crochet cotton, number 10

Hook

size 7

Directions

TO START: Ch 8, sl st to first ch to form ring.

RND 1: Ch 3, work 1 popcorn st in ring, *ch 2, 1 popcorn st in ring, rep from * until 8 popcorn sts are completed. End with ch 2, sl st to center of first popcorn st.

NOTE: See page 17 for directions on popcorn st. Please note that the first ch 3 is included as part of the dcs of first popcorn stitch only. Thereafter work 5 dc for each popcorn st, as indicated in instructions.

RND 2: Sl st up to ch-2 sp, ch 3, 1 popcorn st in same ch-2 sp, ch 2, 1 popcorn st in same ch-2 sp, * ch 2, 2 dc in next ch-2 sp, ch 2, ** 1 popcorn st in next ch-2 sp, ch 2, 1 popcorn st in same ch-2 sp [corner], rep from * 3 times. Rep from * to ** 1 time. End with sl st to first ch-2 sp.

RND 3: Ch 3, work 1 popcorn st in ch-2 corner sp, ch 2, 1 popcorn st in same ch-2 corner sp, * 3 dc in next ch-2 sp, 1 dc in each of next 2 dc, 3 dc in ch 2 sp, ** work 1 popcorn st in ch-2 corner sp, ch 2, 1 popcorn st in same ch-2 corner sp; rep from * 3 times. Rep from * to ** 1 more time. End with sl st to top of first ch 3.

RND 4: Ch 3, 2 dc in ch-2 corner sp, ch 2, 3 dc in same ch-2 corner sp, ch 1, * 1 dc in each of next 4 dc, 1 popcorn st between 4th and 5th dc, 1 dc in each of next 4 dc, ch 1, ** 3 dc in ch-2 corner sp, ch 2, 3 dc in same ch-2 corner sp, ch 1; rep from * 3 times. Rep from * to ** 1 time. End with sl st to top of first ch 3.

RND 5: Sl st up to ch-2 sp, ch 3, 2 dc in ch-2 corner sp, ch 2, 3 dc in same ch-2 corner sp, * ch 1, 1 dc in ch-1 sp, 1 dc in each of next 4 dc, 1 popcorn st on 1 side of previous popcorn st, 1 popcorn st on other side of previous popcorn st, 1 dc on next 4 dc, 1 dc in ch-1 sp, ch 1, ** 3 dc in ch-2 corner sp, ch 2, 3 dc in same ch-2 corner sp; rep from * 3 times. Rep from * to ** 1 time. End with sl st to top of first ch 3.

RND 6: Sl st up to ch-2 sp, ch 3, 1 popcorn st in ch-2 corner sp, ch 2, 1 popcorn st in same ch-2 corner sp, * ch 1, 1 dc in ch-1 sp, 1 dc in each of next 5 dc, 1 popcorn st before, center and after next 2 popcorn sts [3 popcorn sts altogether]; 1 dc in next 5 dc, 1 dc in ch-1 sp, ch 1, ** 1 popcorn st in ch-2 corner sp, ch 2, 1 popcorn st in same ch-2 corner sp, rep from * 3 times. Rep from * to ** 1 time. End with sl st to first ch 3.

RND 7: Sl st up to ch-2 sp, ch 3, 1 popcorn st in

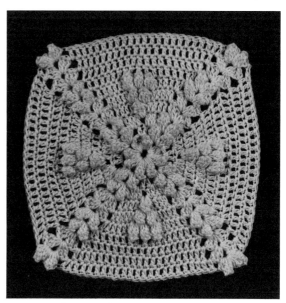

2-20. Raindrop Motif.

ch-2 corner sp, ch 2, 1 popcorn st in same ch-2 corner sp, * ch 1, 1 dc in ch-1 sp, 1 dc in each of next 6 dc, 1 dc on each popcorn st [3 dc altogether], 1 dc in next 6 dc, 1 dc in ch-1 sp, ch 1, ** 1 popcorn st in ch-2 corner sp, ch 2, 1 popcorn st in same ch-2 corner sp; rep from * 3 times. Rep from * to ** 1 time. End with sl st to first ch 3.

RND 8: Sl st up to ch-2 sp, ch 3, 2 dc in ch-2 corner sp, ch 2, 3 dc in same ch-2 corner sp, * ch 1, 1 dc in ch-1 sp, 1 dc in each of next 17 dc, 1 dc in ch-1 sp, ch 1 ** 3 dc in ch-2 corner sp, ch 2, 3 dc in same ch-2 corner sp; rep from * 3 times. Rep from * to ** 1 time. End with ch 1, sl st to top of first ch 3.

RND 9: Work as for previous rnd, except dc on 19 dc instead of 17.

RND 10: Work as for previous rnd, except dc on 21 dc instead of 19. Work corners with 1 popcorn st in ch-2 corner sp, ch 2, 1 popcorn st in same ch-2 corner sp. Fasten off.

RECTANGULAR DOILY

Size
14 by 18 inches

Thread
2 balls (450 yards each) mercerized crochet cotton, number 20

Hook
size 7

Gauge
10 tr = 1 inch
5 rows = 1 inch

Directions
Work 12 Lacy Motifs, according to the directions that follow, and assemble the 12 as directed.

Lacy Motif
TO START: Ch 10, sl st to first ch to form ring.
RND 1: Ch 3, work 4 dc in ring; * ch 3, 5 dc in ring, rep from * until 4 groups of 5 dc are completed. End with ch 3, sl st to top of first ch 3.
RND 2: Ch 3, 1 dc in each of next 4 dc; * 5 dc in corner ch-3 sp, ** 1 dc in each of next 5 dc, rep from * 3 times. Rep from * to ** 1 more time. End with sl st to top of first ch 3.
RND 3: Ch 3, 1 dc in each of next 4 dc, ch 1, * 1 tr and ch 1 in each of next 5 dc of corner, ** 1 dc in each of next 5 dc, ch 1; rep from * 3 times. Rep from * to ** 1 time. End with sl st to top of first dc.
RND 4: Ch 5, 1 dc in 3rd dc of 5-dc group, ch 5, sk 1 dc, 1 dc in next st, * ch 5, 1 dc in 3rd tr of corner, ch 5, ** 1 dc in first dc of 5-dc group, (ch 5, sk 1 dc, 1 dc in next dc); rep between ( ) 2 times. Rep from * 3 times. Rep from * to ** once. End with sl st in 2nd ch of first ch 5.

RND 5: *Make 6 dc and ch 1 in each ch-5 sp to corner; ch 1, 6 dc, ch 2 in ch-5 sp, [corner], 6 dc in next ch-5 sp; rep from * around. End with sl st to first sc.
RND 6: Ch 3, work 1 3-tr cluster st in ch-1 sp, ch 4 [see Note for cluster instructions in ch-1 sp]. * Ch 4, make 4-tr cluster in ch-1 sp, ch 4, 4-tr cluster in ch-1 sp, ch 4, 4-tr cluster in ch-2 corner sp, ch 4, 4-tr cluster st in same ch-2 corner sp. Rep from * around. End with ch 4, sl st to top of first ch 3.
NOTE: Form cluster by working each tr st of cluster up through step 7 [see page 16], thus retaining lp of st on hook. Work the indicated number of tr sts for each cluster, yo hook, and pull through all lps on hook to fasten cluster.
RND 7: Ch 2, *(4 hdc in ch-4 sp, 1 hdc on top of cluster); rep between ( ) 3 times; * work corner as follows: 4 hdc in ch-4 corner sp, ch 4, 4 hdc, 4 dc in same ch-4 corner sp; 1 hdc on top of cluster; ** rep between ( ) 4 times; rep from * 3 times. Rep from * to ** 1 time. End with 4 hdc in next ch-4 sp, sl st to top of first ch 2 to join.
RND 8: (Ch 6, sk 4 hdc, sc in hdc [top of cluster hdc]); rep between ( ) 3 times; * ch 6, 1 sc in ch-4 corner sp, ch 4, 1 sc in same ch-4 sp, ** rep between ( ) 5 times. Rep from * 3 times. Rep from * to ** once. End with ch 6, sc in hdc [top of cluster hdc], ch 6, sl st to top of first ch 6. Fasten off.

Assembling: First Motif
Attach thread in ch-6 sp next to ch-4 sp of corner; ch 3, 3 dc in same ch-6 sp, 4 dc in next ch-6 sp and remaining ch-6 sps across to corner; ch 2, 1 sc in ch-4 corner sp, ch 2, 4 dc in next ch-6 sp and remaining ch-6 sps to next corner. Continue working edges and corners completely around motif. End with ch 2, sl st to top of ch 3. Fasten off.

2-21. The doily is made up of twelve Lacy Motifs.

Assembling: Second Motif
Work as for First Motif, except work only 3 sides of motif. Complete corner and 4 dc in ch-6 sp before attaching to First Motif. *Ch 1, 1 sc in corresponding sp of First Motif; ch 1, 4 dc in next ch-6 sp of Second Motif, rep from * across. End with ch 2, sl st to top of ch 3. Fasten off.

Assembling: Third Motif
Work as for Second Motif. Attach to First Motif.

Assembling: Fourth Motif
Work as for previous motifs (2 and 3), except work only 3 sides including corner. Ch 1, 1 sc in corresponding sp of Second Motif. Ch 1, 4 dc,

ch 2, 1 sc in ch-4 corner sp, ch 2, 4 dc in next ch-6 sp. Attach next side to Third Motif as previously described. End with ch 2, sl st to top of first ch 3. Fasten off.

Continue adding motifs until all 12 are attached. Refer to first 4 motifs in determining how to attach remaining motifs.

Edging
Attach thread to edge with sl st and ch 3 between 2 groups of 4 dc; 3 dc in same sp, * 1 dc in between 2nd and 4th dc of 4-dc group, 4 dc in next sp, rep from * around entire doily. Work corners with 4 dc in each of 2 ch-2 sps. End with sl st to top of first ch 3 to join. Fasten off.

37

2-22. Four squares of Motif A are joined together for the Granny Square Afghan. Designed by Barbara Matheson.

2-23. Square Motif B of the Granny Square Afghan.

GRANNY SQUARE AFGHAN

Size

approximately 48 by 72 inches

Thread

36 skeins (2 ounces each) Luster Sheen by Coats and Clark

Hook

size G

Gauge

4 clusters of 3 dc = 2 inches
4 rows = 2 inches

39

Directions

Work 72 of Square A and 17 of Square B and assemble as directed.

Square A
TO START: Ch 4, join with sl st to form ring.
RND 1: Ch 3, 2 dc into ring, (ch 3, 3 dc in ring) 3 times; ch 3, join to top of first ch 3 with sl st.
RND 2: Sl st in top of next 2 dc and in ch-3 sp, ch 3, 2 dc in same ch-3 sp, ch 3 3 dc in same sp, *(3 dc, ch 3, 3 dc) in next ch-3 corner sp, rep from * around. End with sl st to top of first ch 3 to join.
RND 3: Sl st in top of next dc (ch 3, 4 dc in same dc), drop lp from hook, insert hook from front to back through top of ch 3 and through lp, draw lp through [popcorn stitch completed]. [See Note.] Ch 1, * popcorn st in corner sp, ch 3, popcorn st in same sp, ch 1, popcorn st in center dc of next shell, ch 1, popcorn st in next sp, ch 1, popcorn st in center dc of next shell, ch 1, rep from * around. End with sl st to top of first ch 3 to join.
NOTE: After the first popcorn, all others are done with 5 dcs, omitting the ch 3.
RND 4: Sl st to next ch-1 sp, ch 3, 3 dc in same sp, 3 dc in each of next 4 ch-1 sps, rep from * around. End with sl st to top of first ch 3.
RND 5: Ch 1, sc in same st, sc around square in this manner: Make 1 sc in each dc, 3 sc in each corner sp; join with sl st. Fasten off.
RND 6: Ch 1, sc in same st, sc around square in this manner: Make 1 sc in each dc, 3 sc in each corner sp; join with sl st. Fasten off.

Make 4 small squares in this manner. Join the small squares to make a large square by single crocheting them together. Work from the back with the squares placed right sides together. Fasten off. Join yarn to the center sc of any corner, ch 3, 2 dc in same st, dc around square in this manner: 1 dc in each sc, 3 dc in center sc of each corner sp. End with sl st to top of first ch 3 and fasten off.

Work 18 4-square groups of Square A.

Square B
TO START: Work as for the small squares of Square A, working through Rnd 4.
RND 5: Sl st to next sp between shells, ch 3, 2 dc in same sp, *(3 dc, ch 3, 3 dc in corner sp), 3 dc shell in each sp across, rep from * around. End with sl st to top of ch 1.
RND 6: Rep Rnd 5.
RND 7: Ch 1, 1 sc in front lp of top of same st; sc around in this manner; 2 sc in front lp of top of each dc, 2 sc in front lp of each ch at corners. End with sl st to first ch 1.
RND 8: Ch 1, working only in back lps of same row you worked in Rnd 7; sl st in back lp of same dc, ch 3, 2 dc in same lp, sk 2 lps, 3 dc in next lp. [See Note.] * Sk 2 lps (3 dc in next lp, ch 3 in next lp) rep between ( ) 7 times, rep from * around. End with sl st to top of first ch 3 to join.
NOTE: The shells formed should fall in the sp they would have without the working of Rnd 7, so the granny square pattern remains uninterrupted.
RND 9: Rep Rnd 5.
RND 10: Rep Rnd 5.
RND 11: Ch 3, dc around square in this manner: Make 1 dc in each dc on sides, make 1 dc in first ch st, 3 dc in next ch st, 1 dc in last ch st for corners; join with sl st to top of first ch 3 and fasten off.

Work 17 of Square B.

Assembling
Alternate the 4 square blocks of Square A with the larger Square B blocks and join them together with sl sts. (See diagram.) Join yarn at any point and dc all around the afghan, then add 2 extra rows of dc at each end. Fasten off.

2-24. Assembling the afghan.

ANTIQUE BEDSPREAD

Size

Bedspread: 88 by 110 inches
Motif: 17½ by 17½ inches

Thread

45 balls (200 yards each) bedspread cotton (If not readily available, use crochet cotton number 10 and be aware that your gauge may vary from ours.)

Hook

size 5

Gauge

6 dc = 1 inch
7 rows = 2 inches

Directions

Make 20 motifs and assemble as directed.

Motif
TO START: Ch 6, join with sl st to form ring.
RND 1: Ch 3, 2 tr in ring, * ch 3, 3 tr in ring, rep from * 3 times. End with ch 2, sl st to top of first ch 3 to join.
RND 2: Ch 3, 1 tr in beg ch of ch 3, * 1 tr in each of next 3 tr, (1 tr in each of next 2 ch, ch 3, 1 tr in same last ch, 1 tr in next ch) [corner]; rep from * 4 times. End with ch 3, sl st to top of first ch 3.
RND 3: Ch 3, 1 tr in beg ch of ch 3, * 1 tr in each of next 3 tr, 1 popcorn st in next tr [see page 17 for instructions for popcorn st]; 1 tr in each of next 3 tr; (1 tr in each of next 2 ch, ** ch 3, 1 tr in same last ch, 1 tr in next ch) [corner]; rep from * 3 times. Rep from * to ** 1 time. End with ch 3, sl st to top of first ch 3.
RND 4: Ch 3, 1 tr in beg ch of ch 3, * 1 tr in each of next 3 tr, 1 popcorn st in next tr, 1 tr in next

tr, 1 tr in next tr, 1 tr over previous popcorn st, 1 tr in next tr, 1 popcorn st, 1 tr in each of next 3 tr, 1 tr in each of next 2 ch, ** ch 3, 1 tr in same last ch, 1 tr in next ch; rep from * 3 times. Rep from * to ** 1 time. End with ch 3, sl st to top of first ch 3.
RND 5: Ch 3, 1 tr in beg ch of ch 3, * 1 tr in each of next 3 tr; (1 popcorn st in next tr, 1 tr in next tr, 1 tr in previous popcorn st, 1 tr in next tr) 3 times; 1 tr in each of next 3 tr, 1 tr in each of next 2 ch, ** ch 3, 1 tr in same last ch, 1 tr in next ch; rep from * 3 times. Rep from * to ** 1 time. End with ch 3, sl st to top of first ch 3.
RND 6: Ch 3, 1 tr in beg ch of ch 3, * 1 tr in each of next 3 tr; (1 popcorn st in next tr, 1 tr in next tr, 1 tr in previous popcorn st, 1 tr in next tr) 4 times; 1 tr in each of next 3 tr, 1 tr in each of next 2 ch, ** ch 3, 1 tr in same last ch, 1 tr in next ch; rep from * 3 times. Rep from * to ** 1 time. End with ch 3, sl st to top of first ch 3.
RND 7: Ch 3, 1 tr in beg ch of ch 3, * 1 tr in each of next 3 tr; (1 popcorn st in next tr, 1 tr in next tr, 1 tr in previous popcorn st, 1 tr in next tr) 5 times; 1 tr in each of next 3 tr, 1 tr in each of next 1 ch, ** ch 3, 1 tr in same last ch, 1 tr in next ch; rep from * 3 times. Rep from * to ** 1 time. End with ch 3, sl st to top of first ch 3.
RND 8: Ch 3, 1 tr in beg ch of ch 3, * tr in each of next 3 tr; (1 popcorn st in next tr, 1 tr in next tr, 1 tr in previous popcorn st, 1 tr in next tr) 6 times; 1 tr in each of next 3 tr, 1 tr in each of next 2 ch, ** ch 3, 1 tr in same last ch, 1 tr in next ch; rep from * 3 times. Rep from * to ** once. End with ch 3, sl st to top of first ch 3.
RND 9: Ch 3, 1 tr in beg ch of ch 3 * 1 tr in each of next 7 tr; (1 popcorn st in next tr, 1 tr in next tr, 1 tr in previous popcorn st, 1 tr in next tr) 5 times; 1 tr in each of next 7 tr, 1 tr in each of next 2 ch, ** ch 3, 1 tr in same last ch, 1 tr in next ch; rep from * 3 times. Rep from * to ** 1 time. End with ch 3, sl st to top of first ch 3.

2-25. This antique bedspread, originally crocheted by Tina Bergman in 1920, features a pattern that was popular throughout the later 19th and early 20th centuries. The pattern is actually a combination of treble crochet and popcorn stitches. The large motifs are crocheted separately and then joined together later.

2-26. Detail of one of the motifs from the Antique Bedspread.

RND 10: Ch 3, 1 tr in beg ch of ch 3 * 1 tr in each of next 11 tr; (1 popcorn st in next tr, 1 tr in next tr, 1 tr in previous popcorn st, 1 tr in next tr) 4 times; 1 tr in each of next 11 tr, 1 tr in each of next 2 ch, ** ch 3, 1 tr in same last ch, 1 tr in next ch; rep from * 3 times. Rep from * to ** 1 time. End with ch 3, sl st to top of first ch 3.

RND 11: Ch 3, 1 tr in beg ch of ch 3, * 1 tr in each of next 15 tr; (1 popcorn st in next tr, 1 tr in next tr, 1 tr in previous popcorn st, 1 tr in next tr) 3 times; 1 tr in each of next 15 tr, 1 tr in each of next 2 ch, ** ch 3, 1 tr in same last ch, 1 tr in next ch; rep from * 3 times. Rep from * to ** 1 time. End with ch 2, sl st to top of first ch 3.

RND 12: Ch 3, 1 tr in beg ch of ch 3, * 1 tr in each of next 19 tr; (1 popcorn st in next tr, 1 tr in next tr, 1 tr in previous popcorn st, 1 tr in next tr) 2 times; 1 tr in each of next 19 tr, 1 tr in each of next 2 ch, ** ch 3, 1 tr in same last ch, 1 tr in next ch; rep from * 3 times. Rep from * to ** 1 time. End with ch 3, sl st to top of first ch 3.

RND 13: Ch 3, 1 tr in beg ch of ch 3, * 1 tr in each of next 23 tr; 1 popcorn st in next tr, 1 tr in next tr, 1 tr in previous popcorn st, 1 tr in next tr; 1 tr in each of next 23 tr, 1 tr in each of next 2 ch, ** ch 3, 1 tr in same last ch, 1 tr in next ch; rep from * 3 times. Rep from * to ** 1 time. End with ch 3, sl st to top of first ch 3.

RND 14: Ch 3, 1 tr in beg ch of ch 3; work 1 tr in each st around, working corners as before; end with ch 3, sl st to top of first ch 3.

RND 15: Ch 3, 1 tr in beg ch of ch 3, * sk 1 st, 1 tr in next st, rep from * around working corners as before. End with ch 3, sl st to top of first ch 3.

RND 16: Repeat Rnd 14.

RND 17: Ch 3, 1 tr in beg ch of ch 3, 1 tr in next tr, * 1 popcorn st in next tr, 1 tr in each of next 3 tr, rep from * around working corners as before. End with ch 2, sl st to top of first ch 3.

RND 18: Rep Rnd 17.

RND 19: Rep Rnd 14.

RND 20: Rep Rnd 15.

RND 21: Rep Rnd 14.

RND 22: Ch 3, 1 tr in beg ch of ch 3, * 1 tr in next tr; (1 popcorn st in next tr, 1 tr in each of next 3 tr) 6 times; 1 tr in each of next 39 tr; (1 popcorn st in next tr, 1 tr in each of next 3 tr) 5 times; 1 popcorn st in next tr, 1 tr in next tr (1 tr in each of next 2 ch, ** ch 3, 1 tr in same last ch, 1 tr in next ch) corner; rep from * 3 times. Rep from * to ** once. End with ch 2, sl st to top of first ch 3.

RND 23: Rep Rnd 22, increasing the number of tr on each side to 43 tr.

RND 24: Rep Rnd 22, increasing to 47 tr.

RND 25: Rep Rnd 22, increasing to 51 tr.

RND 26: Rep Rnd 22, increasing to 55 tr.

RND 27: Rep Rnd 22, increasing to 59 tr. Fasten off.

Assembling

Lay out the squares, side by side, 4 squares by 5 squares. Join squares together with a sl st or weave together so that a ridge is not formed on either side. [See page 18 for joining instructions.]

Border

ROW 1: After squares are joined, fasten crochet thread to any corner. Ch 3, work 1 tr in beg ch of ch 3; work 1 tr in each st around, working corners as before. End with ch 2, sl st to top of first ch 3.

ROW 2: Ch 3, 1 tr in beg ch of ch 3, * sk 1 st, 1 tr in next tr, rep from * around, working corners as before. End with ch 2, sl st to top of first ch 3.

ROW 3: Rep Row 1.

ROW 4: Ch 3, 1 tr in beg ch of ch 3, 1 tr in next tr (1 popcorn st, 1 tr in each of next 3 tr) rep between ( ) across entire side of spread, working corners as before. End with ch 2, sl st to top of first ch 3.

ROW 7: Rep Row 1. Fasten off.

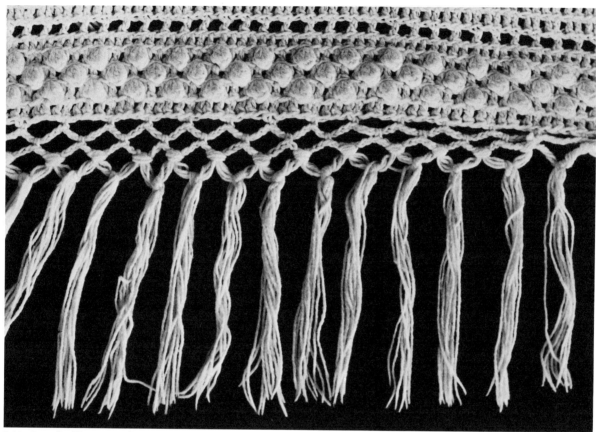

2-27. Detail of fringe on the Antique Bedspread.

Fringe

ROW 1: Fasten thread on either long side of spread. Work 1 sc in next st, ch 5, sk 3 sts, 1 sc in next st, rep from * on 3 sides. Leave top side of spread without fringe.

ROW 2: Turn work, * ch 5, 1 sc in middle of previous ch, rep from * around. Work (Ch 5 and 1 sc into middle of previous ch) 2 times into corners. Fasten off.

For each tassel cut five 13-inch pieces of thread. Take 5 in a group and mount in middle of each ch-5 group. Then take half the threads from each fringe and tie in a square knot. [The square knot is used for joining 2 pieces of thread or yarn securely. It works best when both are of the same thickness. Entwine the thread with both hands and point the ends away from you, left end over and right end under the ropes being joined. Pass the right end over the left end and through the resulting lp. Pull both thread ends to tighten the knot. The finished knot consists of 2 opposing lps that keep each other from slipping.]

2-28. The Tea Cozy is made with six Geometric Pentagon Motifs joined together.

MOTIF TEA COZY

Size
8½ by 7 inches

Thread
2 balls (200 yards each) mercerized crochet cotton, number 10

Hook
size 7

Directions
Crochet the motifs and assemble as directed.

Motifs
Work six Geometric Pentagon Motifs following directions on page 32. This tea cozy was crocheted to fit a particular teapot. It can easily be made to fit any size teapot by repeating the last round as many times as necessary to gain the size desired.

Assembly: First Motif
Work 1 complete motif.

Assembly: Second Motif
Finish motif on 4 sides, including 4th corner. Ch 1, 1 sl st in ch-1 sp of First Motif, ch 1, 3 dc in ch-2 sp of Second Motif, * ch 1, 1 sl st in next ch-1 sp of First Motif, 3 dc in ch-2 sp of Second Motif. Continue along edge, repeating from * up to corner. In ch-2 corner sp, work shell pat for corner. End with ch 1, sl st to top of first ch 3 to join. Fasten off.

Assembly: Third Motif
Rep as for Second Motif. Note where Third Motif is placed and attached. (See diagram.)

Assembly: Fourth Motif
The procedure to attach Fourth Motif is the same as Second and Third. On the Fourth Mo-

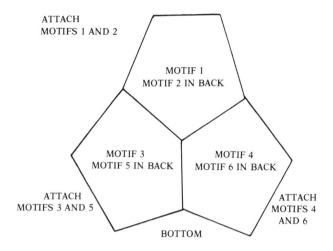

ATTACH
MOTIFS 1 AND 2

MOTIF 1
MOTIF 2 IN BACK

MOTIF 3
MOTIF 5 IN BACK

MOTIF 4
MOTIF 6 IN BACK

ATTACH
MOTIFS 3 AND 5

ATTACH
MOTIFS 4
AND 6

BOTTOM

2-29. Assembling the Motif Tea Cozy (front and back views).

tif, work on 3 sides and leave 2 sides to be attached to Third Motif. Work from the bottom of the cozy to corner. The 3 corners are worked as follows: Work half of corner shell (3 dc, ch 1); 1 sl st in ch-2 sp of Third Motif [corner], ch 1, a sl st in ch-2 sp of Second Motif [corner]; ch 1, 1 sl st to top of first ch 3, complete other half of shell on Fourth Motif to finish corner [3 dc]. Continue attaching Fourth Motif to Second Motif and finish as for Second Motif. One side of cozy is now completed.

Work the other side of the cozy in the same manner as described above. Follow the diagram for progression of motifs. Attach sides of Motifs 3 to 5 and 4 to 6 with sc. With 1 sc in each dc and 1 sc in each ch-1 sp. Attach 2 sides of Motifs 1 and 2. Work 1 sc in each dc and 1 sc in each ch 1 sp. End off.

Finishing
At bottom of tea cozy make 1 dc in each dc and 1 dc in each ch-1 sp. Work (1 dc, ch 1, 1 dc) in next ch-2 sp of corner. (See diagram.)

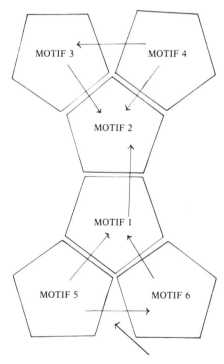

2-30. Assembling the Motif Tea Cozy (flat view).

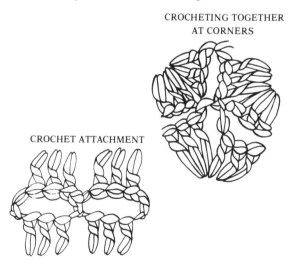

CROCHETING TOGETHER
AT CORNERS

CROCHET ATTACHMENT

2-31. Crocheting the motifs together.

2-32. The elegant Motif Evening Purse is made of seven motifs joined together.

MOTIF EVENING PURSE

Size

7½ by 7½ inches

Thread

2 balls (175 yards each) J. P. Coats Knit-Cro-Sheen

Hook

size 7

Directions

Motifs

Work 7 Fancy Motifs, following directions on page 33.

Assembling

The front of the purse consists of 3 motifs and the back consists of 4. Assemble the back first. Place 2 squares to be joined 1 against the other, wrong sides together. Working on the right side, for each sc, insert hook through both threads of the sts. This gives a slightly ridged effect. Assemble the next 2 squares in the same manner. Now with 2 sets of squares attached, assemble so that the back now is a total of 4 squares. The front is assembled in the same way, except 3 motifs are assembled. Crochet the front to the back, using the same instructions described above.

Opening

Work 1 sc in each st, starting at the top of closure. Do not break off. (See diagram.) The closure lp can be crocheted at the same time by chaining as many sts as needed to reach around the crocheted button easily. Sl st to first sc, ch 1, turn, sc along ch back to the start of the ch. End with sl st. Fasten off. Lp is now completed.

Button

Crochet a ch of approximately 14 inches. Break off. Find the middle of the ch and start to tie it into knots, keeping it in the shape of a ball as you tie. Secure the 2 ends to the center of the purse, as shown in the diagram.

Strap

Attach thread to purse with sl st. Ch to desired length. Attach end to purse with sl st, ch 2, turn, 1 hdc in each ch to end. Sl st to purse, ch 2, turn, 1 hdc in each hdc to end. Sl st to purse. This can be repeated as many times as needed to obtain desired width. Fasten off.

Tassels

Cut out a piece of cardboard 4½ by 3 inches. Wrap crochet thread around cardboard 15 times. [Wrap around 4½-inch side.] Slip thread off cardboard and cut 1 end. Keep the threads folded so a lp is at the top. Insert your crochet hook through the edge of the work on the wrong side and pick up the lp formed at the center of the folded strands. Draw this lp a little way through the work. Pick up the ends of the strands with the hook. Draw the strand right through the lp and tighten the knot. Place the tassels as shown in the diagram.

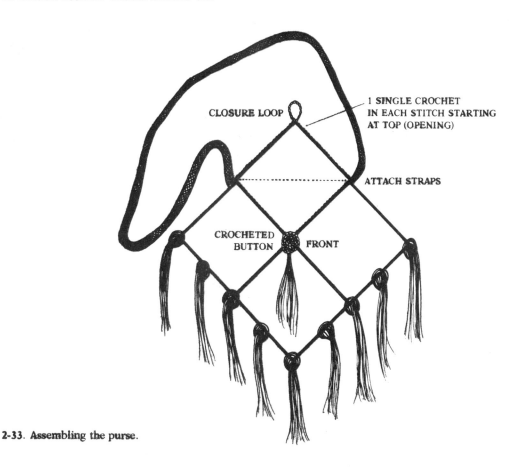

2-33. Assembling the purse.

C H A P T E R   T H R E E

FILET CROCHET

Filet crochet is an open-work technique which was very popular in the early part of the twentieth century. Crocheters worked the filet designs into curtains, bedspreads, table-cloths, and borders for sheets, pillowcases, and towels. The table cover in Figure 3-1 is an example of some intricate filet work.

Although the filet design may look intricate and complicated, it is one of the easier crochet techniques. In fact, it is probably the most free and creative way of crocheting. Filet is accomplished by skipping over one stitch of the previous row and working a chain over it to form a space. The solid portions of the designs are created by filling in these spaces with a double crochet.

Figures 3-2 through 3-6 show examples of fine filet work.

51

3-1. Mrs. Anna Rundquist of Elgin, Illinois, crocheted a white cotton table cover while expecting the birth of her first son. The pattern commemorates the United States Centennial and includes eagles, flags, and shield, as well as the dates 1776 and 1876. The size is 59 by 59 inches. Reproduced with the permission of the Smithsonian Institute. (See page 51.)

3-2. A traditional rose filet doily created by Margaret Kovach.

3-3. This filet handbag was crocheted in dark cotton ecru thread and lined with red cotton. Made by Leontine Ringstrand in 1910.

3-4. A filet pattern for a nightgown top. Made by Tina Bergman.

3-5. A filet bouquet design for a pillow top made of dark ecru cotton. From the collection of Julee Nordin.

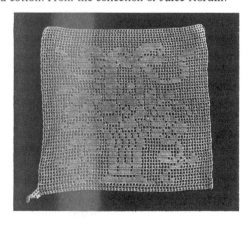

3-6. This intricately patterned antimacassar (armchair cover) features a horse done in solid work against an ornamented open mesh ground. The antimacassar measures 11½ inches square. Reproduced with the permission of the Smithsonian Institute.

UNDERSTANDING GRAPHED DESIGNS

To work a filet mesh design you must follow the graphed design provided in the instructions. Various symbols are used in graphs to indicate where you are to fill in the spaces or leave them blank. The most common symbol, and the one we've used here, is an x. Other pattern sources may use a dot, line, or the space might be darkened. The x resembles the cross-stitch used in embroidery. In fact, you can use cross-stitch embroidery patterns for filet crochet.

Read the pattern graphs for filet crochet, back and forth, starting at the bottom and working row by row. If the pattern graph is perfectly symmetrical, you can read the graph row by row, starting at the right for each row. However, for a nonsymmetrical pattern, you must read it back and forth (right to left, left to right, etc.). Each square of the graph has the symbol for either a space or a fill-in. Filet mesh is usually worked in a double crochet stitch with one chain and a skipped stitch creating the space, and a double crochet in the next two stitches to create solid areas.

In other words:

1 open mesh □ = 1 dc, ch 1, sk 1 st of previous row

1 solid mesh ⊠ = 1 dc in dc of previous row, 1 dc in ch-1 sp

However, if you desire a fuller, heavier texture to your work, the double mesh crochet stitch should be used instead of the regular double crochet. This stitch gives more definition to the design. It is worked in a slightly different manner than the regular double crochet stitch as follows:

Yo hook, insert hook in next ch, pull thread through 3 lps on hook, yo hook and pull thread through only 1 ch, yo hook and draw through 3 remaining chs on hook.

54

WORKING THE DESIGN

Usually the pattern instructions indicate how many stitches the foundation chain should have. However, there is a rule of thumb for determining this yourself. Count the number of squares in Row 1 of the graph. Multiply by 2. To this number add 6 chain stitches.

for example:

$$\begin{array}{r} 30 \text{ squares across Row 1 of graph} \\ \times\ 2 \\ \hline 60 \\ +\ 6 \\ \hline 66 \text{ foundation chains} \end{array}$$

Once you've decided upon the appropriate number of chains, work the first row as follows:

Beginning in the 6th ch from hook, work 1 dc *ch 1, sk 1 ch, work 1 dc * rep from * across, ch 5, and turn work.

Now just follow the graph row by row. Whenever a space is filled in on the graph then you must work a double crochet into that space rather than the chain 1, skip 1 stitch, as for the open areas. Remember to chain 5 and turn work at the end of each row on the graph. Note that the chain 5 is intended only as a guide. In actuality, the chain stitches needed to turn the work will vary according to the crocheter. Some crocheters work more loosely or tightly than others. Thus you may have to adjust the number of chains to suit your own work. It is important to use just the right number of chains in order to make the edge of the work square. Too many turning chains, for example, will cause the edge of the work to become wavy; whereas too few turning chains will cause the work to pull.

DESIGNING ORIGINAL PATTERNS

It's easy to design your own pattern graphs. You'll need some 10-squares-to-the-inch graph paper, but if you can't find any, with some patience, a pencil, and a ruler, you can make your own graph paper. Another alternative is to use the half-space on your typewriter and type it out. Once you have a master copy of whatever graph paper you've come by, xerox or duplicate several more.

When you have decided on your design, outline and pencil it in directly onto the graph paper. Then "X in" the solid parts, following your outline. Some designers x their design in directly without using a preliminary outline. Avoid the temptation to use the whole sheet of graph paper for your design unless you want a larger work. Remember, too, that the resulting size of the work will to a large degree depend upon the size hook and thread you are using. Much more design detail is possible with smaller hooks and finer threads. But also remember that the hook must be compatible with the thread. Some threads are too coarse for finer hooks. For example, size 10 thread is not suited to a 14 hook. It is a good idea to work a small sample of the design with several sizes of hooks and threads.

FINISHING THE WORK

After your crochet work is finished, it may require an outside edge to give it body and to prevent stretching. Slip stitch or single crochet (see page 14) around the outside edge of the piece; for other edgings, see Chapter 6.

Blocking is necessary to acquire the proper size, to make the piece lay flat, and to give it a neat, pressed appearance. The idea is to moisten the piece so that it will give when you pull it to shape, and then apply heat to fix its new shape. The moistening can be done in either of two ways. You can either spray with water or use a damp cloth. Spraying can be done with a mister (such as you might use for your plants). In any case, you must always use an iron set at medium heat. Press to size as you iron. If you use a damp cloth, place the cloth over the piece and press lightly with the iron. Make sure you distribute even weight as you iron, and don't let the iron stand still in any one place. Take your time to acquire the size intended and, most importantly, make sure the iron doesn't get too hot! You wouldn't want your work to scorch.

Keep blocking until all edges are neat and even, and allow to dry thoroughly.

BUTTERFLY SACHET PILLOW

Size

5 by 2¾ inches

Materials

1 ball (250 yards) mercerized crochet cotton, number 30
2 pieces velvet or satin, 5½ by 3 inches
sewing thread to match
sewing needle
a favorite dusting powder or potpourri for scent

Hook

size 10

Gauge

15 dc = 1 inch
7 rows = 1 inch

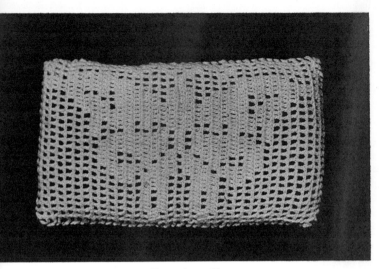

3-7. Butterfly Sachet Pillow.

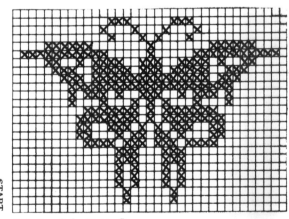

START

3-8. Graph for Butterfly.

Directions

Follow the filet crochet directions at the beg of the chapter and work the project as follows.

Filet Work

TO START: Ch 56. Dc in 6th ch from hook, *ch 1, sk 1 ch, dc in next ch, rep from * across till

56

end of ch. Dc in last ch and ch 6. Turn. You now have completed Row 1 of the design, which is a row of open mesh. Continue for Row 2 and subsequent rows, following the graph, and filling in each solid mesh with 2 dc. Be sure to keep motif square and even. Always ch 6 to turn and end the rows with 1 dc in 3rd ch of ch 6.

TO FINISH: Block the piece carefully, following the directions at the beg of the chapter.

Assembly

You are now ready to assemble the pillow. Follow the diagram. Take the 2 pieces of velvet or satin, with right sides facing, and sew, either

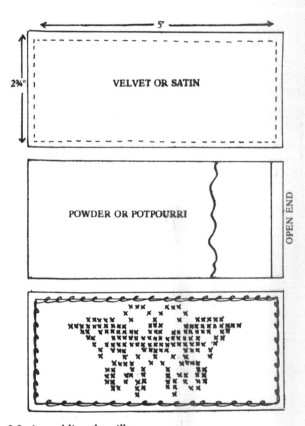

3-9. Assembling the pillow.

by hand or machine, around 2 long sides and 1 short. Leave 1 end open; turn pillow right side out. A light steam pressing may be necessary. Fill the pillow with any kind of scent you desire. After you have filled it ¾ full, hand-sew the end with a whip stitch. (Be sure to use very small sts.) The butterfly filet design is sewn directly on the pillow with a whip stitch also. Sew only around the outside of the butterfly.

You can keep your pillow in your dresser drawer or put a string through the corner and slip it over a hanger in your closet. The sachet pillow will keep your clothes smelling fresh and clean.

EGGBEATER WINDOW HANGING

Size
6 by 16 inches

Materials
1 ball (450 yards) mercerized crochet cotton, number 20

Hook
size 10

Gauge
10 dc = 1 inch
5 rows = 1 inch

Directions
Follow the filet crochet directions at the beg of the chapter and work the project as follows.

Filet Work
TO START: Ch 66. Dc in 6th ch from hook. *Ch 1, sk 1 ch and dc in next. Rep from * until end of

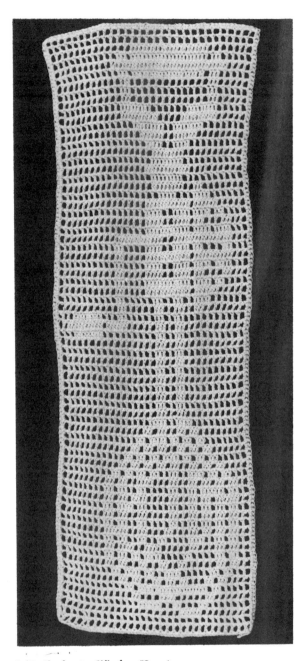

3-10. Eggbeater Window Hanging.

ch. When completed there should be 30 squares for the base of the hanging. Ch 6, turn, and continue dc on top of next. Follow graph, row by row. Where there is a filled sp, put 1 dc in that sp and a dc on top of next dc. When you come to the end of the row, be careful to dc in 3rd ch of the 6th ch made [turn ch]. This will keep the hanging even on all sides.

TO FINISH: Block the hanging, following directions at the beg of this chapter.

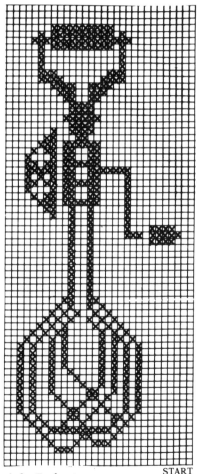

3-11. Graph for Eggbeater.   START

58

Assembly

If you would like to hang your crochet work in the window, just put up either nails or tacks and hang your work. Make sure the hanging is taut so that you can see the entire design. Now it's time to enjoy your creation.

KITCHEN UTENSILS WINDOW HANGING

Size

10 by 11 inches

Materials

1 ball (450 yards) mercerized crochet cotton, number 20

Hook

size 10

Gauge

10 dc = 1 inch
5 rows = 1 inch

Directions

Follow the filet crochet directions at the beg of the chapter and work the project as follows.

Filet Work

TO START: Ch 114. Dc in 6th ch from hook, * ch 1, sk 1 ch and dc in next ch. Rep from * until the end of the ch. When finished there should be 54 squares that make up the base of the hanging. Watch the graph to reassure yourself. From this point, follow graph row by row. Where there is a filled sp, put 1 dc in that sp and 1 dc on top of next dc. Be careful to count the number of sps filled. Also be careful to dc in the 3rd ch of the 6th ch made at the end of each row

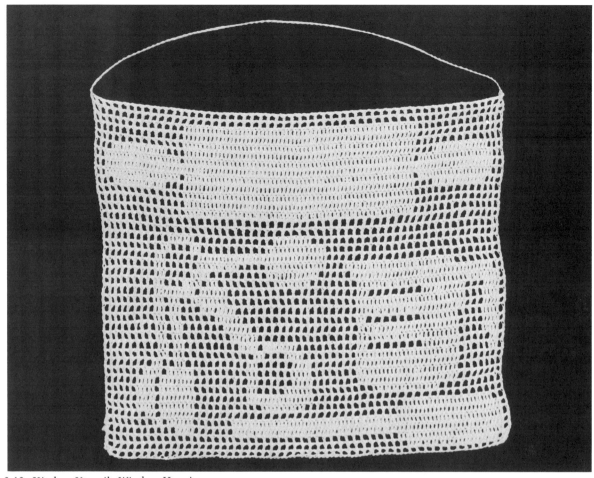

3-12. Kitchen Utensils Window Hanging.

[the turn ch]. This will keep the hanging even on all sides.

TO FINISH: Block the hanging carefully, following the instructions at the beg of the chapter.

Assembly

If you would like to hang your crochet work in the window, just put up either nails or tacks and hang your work. Make sure the hanging is taut so that you can see the entire design.

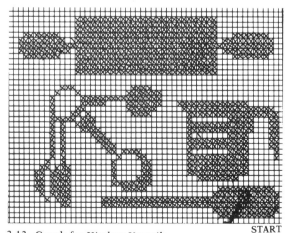

START

3-13. Graph for Kitchen Utensils.

59

3-14. Daffodils Centerpiece.

3-15. Graph for Daffodils.

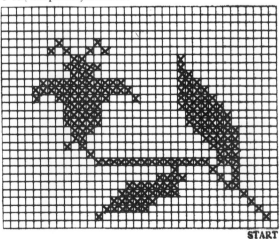

START

DAFFODILS CENTERPIECE

Size
18 by 18 inches

Materials
2 balls (400 yards each) mercerized crochet cotton, number 10

Hook
size 7

Gauge
10 dc = 1 inch
5 rows = 1 inch

Directions
Four motifs are to be made separately and then crocheted tog later. Follow the filet crochet directions at the beg of the chapter and work the project as follows.

Filet Work
TO START: Ch. 70. Dc in 6th ch from hook, *ch 1, sk 1 ch, dc in next dc, rep from * across to the end of the ch. Dc in last ch and ch 6 to turn. [Always ch 6 to turn and in remaining rows dc in 3rd ch of ch 6 in order to keep the end even.] Please note that the daffodil design is worked entirely in double mesh crochet. [See instructions on page 54.] Again, only the fill-in areas are worked in double mesh crochet; the sps are worked in dc as usual. Follow the graph until decs are made at the center.

To *dc at corners of motif:* Follow the design and dc where graph shows beg of decs. When dec at the end of your work, simply do not crochet in the last square; ch 1, to turn. Sl st along top of next square until you reach the top of the next dc, ch 6, and dc in next dc. Continue to

60

follow graph and dec as stated until all decs are made at the 1 corner. Be sure to follow the diagram.

Assembly

When 4 motifs are completed, block each, following blocking instructions on page 18. Prepare to connect all 4 motifs. Motifs are connected by crochet rather than sewing. Crocheting will keep the centerpiece flat and will eliminate puckering after laundering. Be sure to follow the diagram.

Lace Border

After all 4 motifs are connected, it is time to add the Lace Border. First, attach thread to any corner and proceed as follows:

ROW 1: Ch 4 *yo hook, insert hook as shown in diagram. Complete dc across row. Rep from * around to the straight edge of motif. From this point, yo hook, * insert hook into the top of dc, complete dc, ch 1, yo hook, rep from * around.

ROW 2: Ch 4, turn [solid blocks now made]. Dc in sp, *dc on top of dc, rep from * around. Ch 1 and sl st in 3rd ch of ch 4.

ROW 3: Ch 4, turn [sp now made]. Dc in next dc, ch 1, sk 1 dc and dc in next dc [lps now made].

ROW 4: Sc in next sp, *ch 3, sc in next sp, rep from * around.

ROW 5: Ch 3, turn [beg of shell pat]. In lp make 2 hdc, ch 1, 2 hdc, *sc in next lp, 2 hdc, ch 1, 2 hdc in next lp, rep from * around.

ROW 6: Ch 4, turn. In ch-1 sp, 2 hdc, ch 1, 3 hdc, *sc in sc, 2 hdc, ch 1, 2 hdc, rep from * around.

ROW 7: Rep shell pat once more [Row 6].

ROW 8: Ch 3, turn. Make 2 sc, 4 hdc, 2 sc, in ch-1 sp, * sc in sc, 2 sc, 4 hdc, 2 sc, rep from * around. Sl st to first sc to finish. Lace border is now completed.

Block the centerpiece, following instructions at the beg of the chapter.

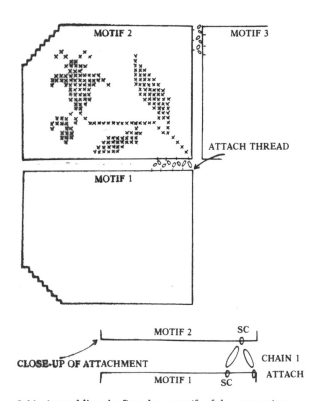

3-16. Assembling the first three motifs of the centerpiece.

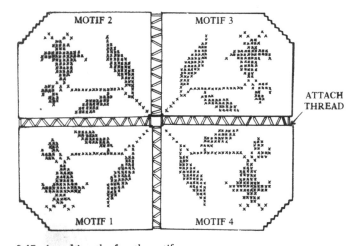

3-17. Attaching the fourth motif.

3-18. Sunflowers Window Cover.

SUNFLOWERS WINDOW COVER

Size
25 by 29 inches

Materials
2 balls (400 yards each) mercerized crochet cotton, number 10

Hook
size 10

Gauge
7 dc = 1 inch
4 rows = 1 inch

Directions
Follow the filet crochet directions at the beg of the chapter and work the project as follows.

Filet Work
TO START: Ch 168 to start. Dc in 6th ch from hook. Continue row by row for 5 rows, follow-ing the graph. The vase portion is done in dc only. The sunflowers are all done in double mesh crochet. [Read instructions at the beg of the chapter to complete double mesh crochet.] The double mesh crochet st gives a fuller, heavier texture to the window cover. Follow the graph carefully. Keep sides even and squared. There are 5 rows of crochet on both top and bottom. There are 10 sps on side of pat. In order to obtain the size you need to exactly fit the window you are covering, continue cro-cheting around the outside of the finished piece of work until it measures correctly. In this way you can custom-make your window cover.

TO FINISH: Now you can block your work. Please read instructions at the beg of the chap-ter on how to block.

Assembly
After blocking your work, put your window cover onto a curtain rod. Take the rod and weave it through the sps at the top of the cover.

3-19. Graph for Sunflowers.

START

62

If the cover is hung like this, it will not droop or sag. The window cover can be washed with mild detergent. Let it drip dry, press, and hang. It will last for a very long time with minimal care.

AMOUR BOOKMARK

Size
2 by 9 inches

Materials
1 ball (250 yards) mercerized crochet cotton, number 30

Hook
size 10

Gauge
17 dc = 1 inch
7 rows = 1 inch

Directions
Follow the filet crochet directions at the beg of the chapter and work the project as follows.

Filet Work
TO START: Ch 32. Dc in 6th ch from hook. *Sk 1 ch, 1 dc in next st, rep from * across. End with ch 1, 1 dc in 3rd ch of ch 6. On all remaining ch turns, ch only 5 to turn, sk 2 chs of 5 ch and 1 dc in next ch. Follow graph for remainder of piece.
TO FINISH: The piece should be steam-pressed later.

Edging
Sc around entire bookmark. Use 2 sc in each ch-1 sp, 3 sc in corners. End with sl st to first sc. Fasten off.

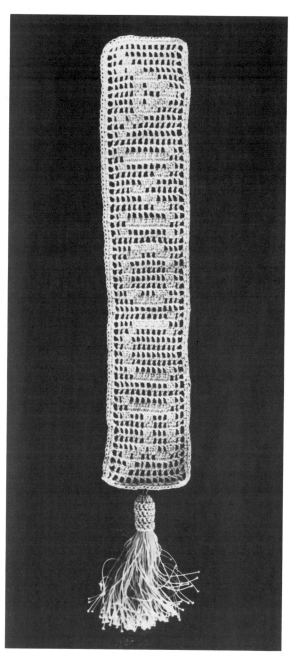
3-20. Amour Bookmark.

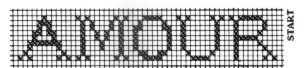

3-21. Graph for Amour.

Tassel Cap

The tassel is attached to center bottom edge of bookmark. Ch 5, sl st to first ch to form ring. Ch 2, 15 hdc in ring. Do not sl st to first ch. Continue working 1 hdc in each hdc until the cap measures approximately ½ inch. Fasten off.

Tassel Fringe

Wrap thread around 3½-inch cardboard square. Wrap around about 60 times. Slip off cardboard and cut 1 end with scissors. With a piece of thread 5 inches long, tie a knot at the top of the tassel fringe. With crochet hook, pull the 2 ends of thread through the cap and through ch-5 ring. Pull cap down evenly over the top of tassel fringe. Two ends of the thread can be used to secure the tassel to the body of the bookmark.

Steam press the bookmark with medium heat.

Spell out any messages you wish for additional bookmarks. [See alphabet.]

3-22. Graph for alphabet. Spell out any message you want by using these letters.

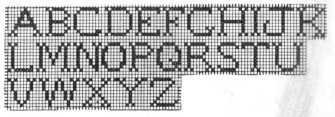

64

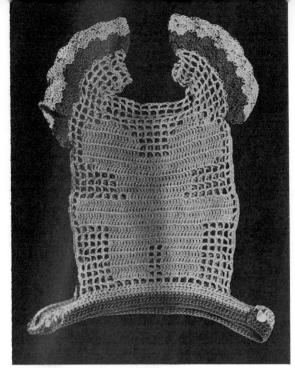

3-23. Teddy Bear Top. Designed by Kathy Uren.

TEDDY BEAR TOP

Size

children's sizes 3 to 4

Materials

2 balls (175 yards each) Coats and Clark Knit-Cro-Sheen in Main Color (MC)
small amount in Colors A and B
two ⅝-inch diameter buttons

Hook

size 2

Gauge

5 sc = 1 inch	3 dc = 1 inch
8 rows = 1 inch	3 rows = 1 inch

Directions

Make each part of the top separately and then assemble.

Back Waistband

TO START: Beginning at Waistband with Color A, ch 85.

ROW 1: Beginning at 2nd ch from hook, 1 sc in each ch across. End with ch 1, turn.

ROWS 2–4: Make 1 sc in each sc across. End with ch 1, turn. Fasten off Color A.

ROW 5 (buttonhole row): Attach Color B and work 1 sc in each of next 4 sc, ch 2, sk 2 sc, continue across row with 1 sc in each sc up to last 6 sts; ch 2, sk 2 sc, 1 sc in each of last 4 sts. End with ch 1, turn.

ROW 6: Make 1 sc in each sc across with 1 sc in each ch over buttonhole. End with ch 1, turn.

ROW 7: Make 1 sc in each sc across. End with ch 1, turn. Fasten off Color B.

Back Body

Sk 22 sc, attach MC thread, ch 5, sk 1 sc, 1 dc in next st, * rep from * to last 21 sts, ch 5, turn.

NEXT ROW: Sk 2 chs, 1 dc in next dc, rep from * across. End with 1 dc in 3rd ch of ch 5, turning ch.

Rep this row until piece measures 10 inches or desired length from beginning.

NEXT ROW (shoulder strap): Ch 5, turn, 1 dc in next dc, ch 2 dc in each of next 4 dc, ch 5, turn.

Rep this row 5 times. Fasten off. Sk 9 sts and attach thread and work 2nd strap the same as first on last 5 stitches. Fasten off.

Front Waistband

Ch 65, work as for Back Waistband, except eliminating buttonholes.

Front Body (Filet Work)

Sk 12 sts on Waistband, attach MC, ch 5, sk 1 sc, 1 dc in next sc, * ch 2, sk 1 sc, 1 dc in next sc, rep from * to last 12 sts. End with ch 5, turn. Follow graph. Complete Shoulder Straps the same as for Back.

Assembly

Sew shoulder seams using same thread and a

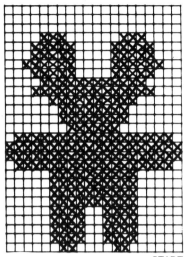

3-24. Graph for Teddy Bear. START

whip stitch. Attach MC to side edge to front side edge where it joins the Waistband, work along side edge of Front and Shoulder Straps and side edge back in sc, working 2 sc in each square and 1 sc in each post. Rep on other side.

To attach ruffled sleeves: Attach Color A to 11th square down from shoulder seam, sc in same sp, * ch 1, sk next sc, 1 sc in next sc, ch 1, sk 1 sc, ch 1, work 5 dc in next sc [shell made], work from * across for 22 squares [17 shells made]. Ch 1, turn.

ROW 2: Sl st in first 2 dc, 1 sc in center st of shell, ch 1, 5 dc in next sc, * ch 1, 1 sc in center st of shell, ch 1, 5 dc in next sc, rep from * across ending in center stitch of last shell with a sl st [16 shells].

ROW 3: Rep Row 2 [15 shells].

ROW 4: Attach Color B and rep Row 2 with Color B [14 shells].

ROW 5: Rep Row 2 [13 shells].

ROW 6: Rep Row 2 [12 shells]. End off with Color B. Complete other Sleeve in same manner.

IRISH CROCHET

Irish crochet is a distinct type of crocheted lace that never goes out of style. It is easily distinguishable from other types of crochet work in that it is three-dimensional. Irish crochet is not worked in rows like ordinary crochet, but instead in a mesh background. Motifs, such as a rose, leaf, or shamrock, are worked separately. The mesh is worked in and around the motifs or the motifs are applied to the mesh. The border of the jabot in Figure 4-1 is a good example of how Irish crochet is used.

According to the National Museum of Ireland, crochet work was first introduced in a convent in the early nineteenth century, and, in an attempt to alleviate some of the dire poverty at the time of the Great Famine (1845 – 1847), crochet centers were started throughout the south of Ireland, the majority of which were in convents. Pupils of the nuns made crocheted articles, sold them, and the proceeds went to relieve some of the suffering. By the 1860s 12,000 women were crocheting in the Cork area.

Another nucleus of the crochet industry was at Thornton, County Kildare, where a Mrs. W. C. Roberts taught the poor of her area the craft of knitting. In 1847, in an effort to spread her work, she began to train women as crochet teachers. Twenty-four of these women went to different parts of the country and one of the teachers was invited by the wife of the rector at Clones in Monaghan County to start a school there. The Clones School grew to be one of the most important crochet centers in the country.

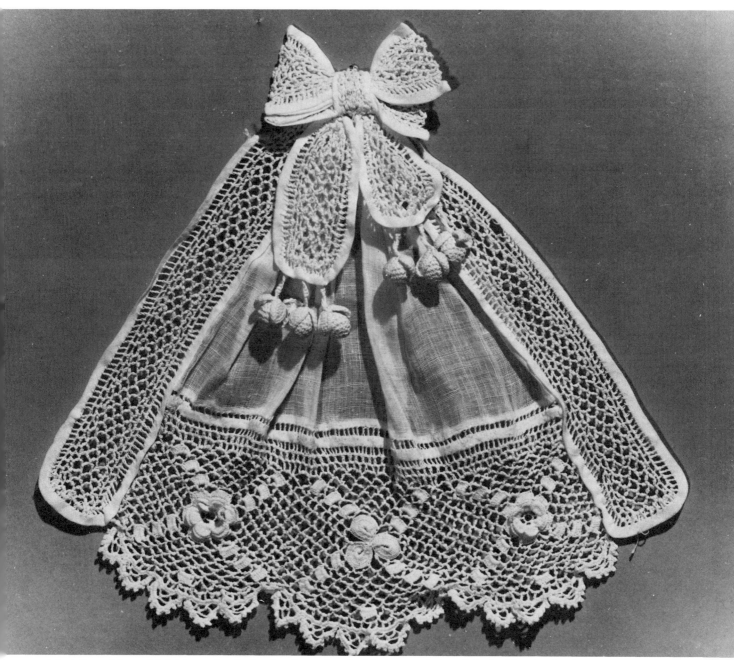

4-1. A linen jabot with Irish crochet in border. Reproduced with the permission of the Smithsonian Institute.

4-2. Two pillowcases with Irish crochet trim and an insertion of a technique known as Mexican drawn work. The pillowcases were made by Edith Olin of Kingsville, Ohio, for her trousseau, circa 1880. Reproduced with the permission of Smithsonian Institute.

4-3. A white cotton parasol, 34 inches in diameter, from the early 20th century. Reproduced with the permission of the Smithsonian Institute.

4-4. A camisole top of the late 19th century. Reproduced with the permission of the Smithsonian Institute.

4-5. Samples of crochet lace from the Clones School, 1880 to 1910. Reproduced with the permission of the National Museum of Ireland, Dublin, Ireland.

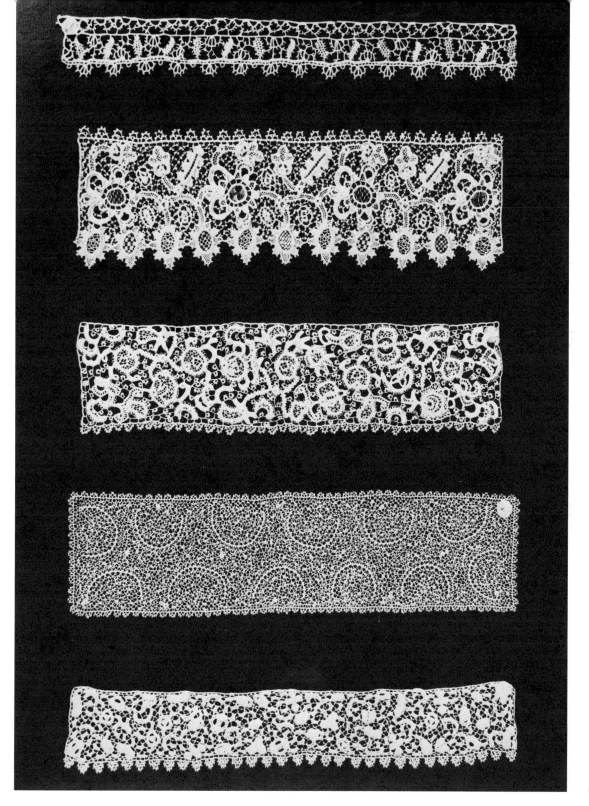

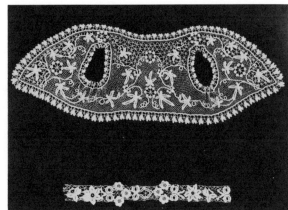

4-6. Samples of work done at the Convent Tralee, Ireland, circa 1912. Reproduced with the permission of the National Museum of Ireland, Dublin, Ireland.

4-7. A Youghal crochet dress made in Ireland, circa 1906 to 1908. Reproduced with the permission of the National Museum of Ireland, Dublin, Ireland.

4-8. Two crochet collars crocheted at the Crawford Municipal School of Art, Ireland, circa 1912. Reproduced with the permission of the National Museum of Ireland, Dublin, Ireland.

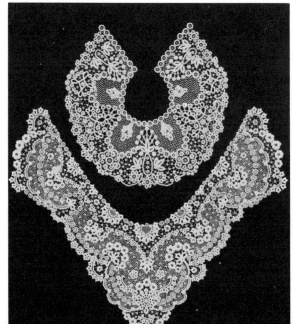

MAKING THE BASIC ROSETTE

The rose or rosette (see Figure 4-9) is the most popular of all Irish Crochet motifs with the leaf and shamrock also being used a great deal. Patterns for the motifs vary greatly from book to book, but basically the look is the same.

TO START: Ch 6, sl st to form ring.

RND 1: Ch 3, 2 dc into ring, (ch 3, 3 dc in ring) rep between ( ) 3 times. End with ch 3, sl st to top of first ch 3 to join.

RND 2: * In next sp, work 1 sc, 5 dc, 1 sc, rep from * around. End with sl st to first sc to join.

RND 3: Ch 5, * sk petal, sl st to first sc of next petal, rep from * around.

RND 4: * In each ch-5 sp, work 1 sc, 7 dc, 1 sc, rep from * around. End with sl st to first sc of first petal to join. Fasten off.

MAKING THE BASIC PANSY

The pansy motif (see Figure 4-10) is a very popular flower design used on a variety of articles. It can be found on doilies, collars and cuffs of dresses and blouses, and on yokes, etc.

TO START: Ch 6, sl st to form ring.

RND 1: Ch 3, 2 dc into ring, (ch 3, 3 dc in ring), rep between ( ) 3 times. End with ch 3, sl st to top of first ch 3 to join.

RND 2: *In next sp, work 13 tr, rep from * around. End with sl st to first tr of first petal. Fasten off.

MAKING THE BACKGROUND NETTING

Irish crochet motifs are attached to a net background. The motifs are crocheted separately and then the net background is crocheted

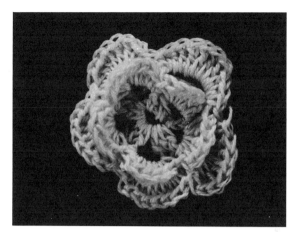

4-9. The Basic Rosette.

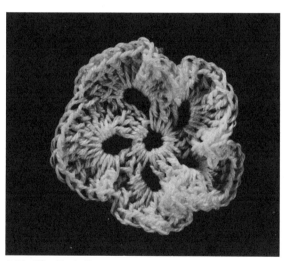

4-10. The Basic Pansy.

around the motifs. The background pattern is not precise, and the intricacy of it depends largely upon the experience of the crocheter as well as the motifs used.

After all of the motifs have been made, they are basted onto whatever area you want your

71

netting to cover, such as collars, cuffs, yokes, etc. The way the motifs are situated is up to you. The article to be decorated should first be prepared.

Crochet a ch to a desired length—one that will go completely around the edge of an article. Then sew this ch onto the fabric with small whip stitches. Neatness is a must. After this is completed, attach thread to any point with a sl st. Then:

*Ch 6, sk several chs [on fabric] and work 1 sc in a ch, ch 6 [or 5 or 7 or 8]; a variation is desired with this netting. Rep from * around article.

On subsequent rows attach with 1 dc to arc created by previous row. This process will bring you to a motif. Catch points of motif with single crochets as you work around. [See diagram.]

A fancier netting can be created with picots. Follow directions for netting above, but substitute a picot for the double crochet. Work the picot as follows:

Ch 6, make 1 sc in first ch of ch 6.

4-11. The background netting.

START

72

ANTIQUE PINWHEEL DOILY WITH IRISH CROCHET EDGING

Size

13 inches in diameter

Materials

1 ball (250 yards) mercerized crochet cotton, number 30
small amounts of variegated thread in blue, red, orange, brown, apricot, yellow, and pink

Hook

size 11

Directions

Study Figure 4-12. Make the doily first and then do the Irish crochet edging.

Doily

TO START: Ch 8, sl st to form ring, ch 5.

RND 1: Work 29 tr into ring. End with sl st to top of ch 5 to join.

RND 2: Ch 5, sk 1 tr, * 1 tr into next tr, sk 1 tr, ch 2, rep from * around. End with sl st to 3rd ch of first ch 5 to join.

RND 3: Ch 5, * 1 tr in next ch-2 sp, 1 tr in next tr, ch 2, rep from * around. End with 1 tr in last ch-2 sp, sl st to 3rd ch of first ch 5 to join.

RND 4: Ch 5, * 1 tr in next ch-2 sp, 1 tr in each of next 2 tr, ch 2, rep from * around. End with 1 tr in last ch-2 sp, 1 tr in last tr, sl st to 3rd ch of first ch 5 to join.

RND 5: Ch 5, * 1 tr in next ch-2 sp, 1 tr in each of next 3 tr, ch 2, rep from * around. End with 1 tr in last ch-2 sp, 1 tr in each of last 2 tr, sl st to 3rd ch of first ch 5 to join.

RND 6: Ch 5, * 1 tr in next ch-2 sp, 1 tr in each of next 4 tr, ch 2, rep from * around. End with 1 tr in last ch-2 sp, 1 tr in each of last 3 tr, sl st to 3rd ch of first ch 5 to join.

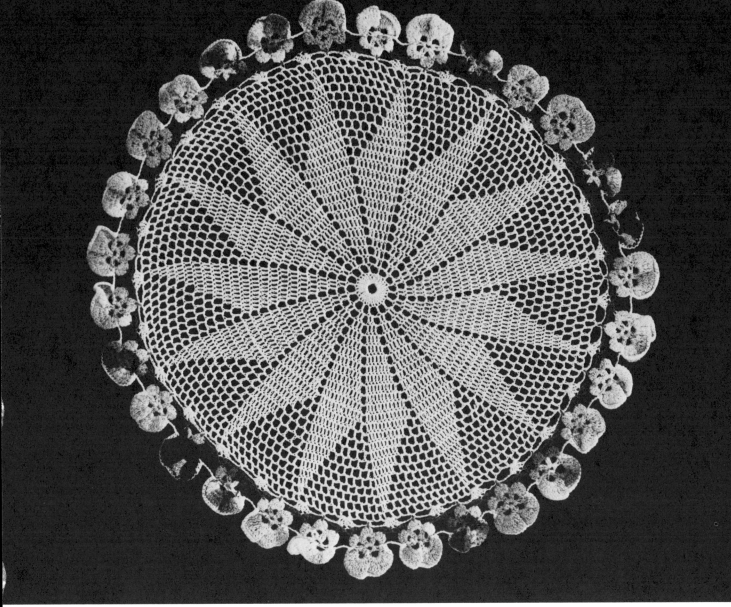

4-12. Antique Pinwheel Doily With Irish Crochet Edging. From the collection of Irma Hitesman.

RND 7: Ch 5, * 1 tr in next ch-2 sp, 1 tr in each of next 5 tr, ch 2, rep from * around. End with 1 tr in last ch-2 sp, rep from * around. End with 1 tr in last ch-2 sp, 1 tr in each of last 4 tr, sl st to 3rd ch of first ch 5 to join.

RND 8: Ch 5, * 1 tr in next ch-2 sp, 1 tr in each of next 6 tr, ch 2, rep from * around. End with 1 tr in last ch-2 sp, 1 tr in each of last 5 tr, sl st to 3rd ch of first ch 5 to join.

RND 9: Ch 5, * 1 tr in next ch-2 sp, 1 tr in each

of next 7 tr, ch 2, rep from * around. End with 1 tr in last ch-2 sp, 1 tr in each of last 6 tr, sl st to 3rd ch of first ch 5 to join.

RND 10: Ch 5, * 1 tr in next ch-2 sp, 1 tr in each of next 8 tr, ch 2, rep from * around. End with 1 tr in last ch-2 sp, 1 tr in each of last 7 tr, sl st to 3rd ch of first ch 5 to join.

RND 11: Ch 5, * 1 tr in next ch-2 sp, 1 tr in each of next 9 tr, ch 2, rep from * around. End with 1 tr in last ch-2 sp, 1 tr in each of last 8 tr, sl st to 3rd ch of first ch 5 to join.

RND 12: Ch 5, * 1 tr in next ch-2 sp, 1 tr in each of next 10 tr, ch 2, rep from * around. End with 1 tr in last ch-2 sp, 1 tr in each of last 9 tr, sl st to 3rd ch of first ch 5 to join.

RND 13: Ch 5, * 1 tr in next ch-2 sp, 1 tr in each of next 11 tr, ch 2, rep from * around. End with 1 tr in last ch-2 sp, 1 tr in each of last 10 tr, sl st to 3rd ch of first ch 5 to join.

RND 14: Ch 5, * 1 tr in next ch-2 sp, ch 2, sk 1 tr, 1 tr in each of next 11 tr, ch 2, rep from * around. End with 1 tr in next ch-2 sp, ch 2, sk 1 tr, 1 tr in each of next 10 tr, sl st to 3rd ch of first ch 5 to join.

RND 15: Ch 5, * (1 tr in next ch-2 sp, ch 2) 2 times; sk 1 tr, 1 tr in each of next 10 tr, ch 2, rep from * around. End with (1 tr in next ch-2 sp, ch 2) 2 times; sk 1 tr, 1 tr in each of next 9 tr, sl st to 3rd ch of first ch 5 to join.

RND 16: Ch 5, * (1 tr in next ch-2 sp, ch 2) 3 times; sk 1 tr, 1 tr in each of next 9 tr, ch 2, rep from * around. End with (1 tr in next ch-2 sp, ch 2) 3 times; sk 1 tr, 1 tr in each of next 8 tr, sl st to 3rd ch of first ch 5 to join.

RND 17: Ch 5, * (1 tr in next ch-2 sp, ch 2,) 4 times; sk 1 tr, 1 tr in each of next 8 tr, ch 2, rep from * around. End with (1 tr in next ch-2 sp, ch 2) 4 times; sk 1 tr, 1 tr in each of next 7 tr, sl st to 3rd ch of first ch 5 to join.

RND 18: Ch 5, * (1 tr in next ch-2 sp, ch 2) 5 times; sk 1 tr, 1 tr in each of next 7 tr, ch 2, rep from * around. End with (1 tr in next ch-2 sp, ch 2) 5 times; sk 1 tr, 1 tr in each of next 6 tr, sl st to 3rd ch of first ch 5 to join.

RND 19: Ch 5, * (1 tr in next ch-2 sp, ch 2) 6 times; sk 1 tr, 1 tr in each of next 6 tr, ch 2, rep from * around. End with (1 tr in next ch-2 sp, ch 2) 6 times; sk 1 tr, 1 tr in each of next 5 tr, sl st to 3rd ch of first ch 5 to join.

RND 20: Ch 5, * (1 tr in next ch-2 sp, ch 2) 7 times; sk 1 tr, 1 tr in each of next 5 tr, ch 2, rep from * around. End with (1 tr in next ch-2 sp, ch 2) 7 times; sk 1 tr, 1 tr in each of next 4 tr, sl st to 3rd ch of first ch 5 to join.

RND 21: Ch 5, * (1 tr in next ch-2 sp, ch 2) 8 times; sk 1 tr, 1 tr in each of next 4 tr, ch 2, rep from * around. End with (1 tr in next ch-2 sp, ch 2) 8 times; sk 1 tr, 1 tr in each of next 3 tr, sl st to 3rd ch of first ch 5 to join.

RND 22: Ch 5, * (1 tr in next ch-2 sp, ch 2) 9 times; sk 1 tr, 1 tr in each of next 3 tr, ch 2, rep from * around. End with (1 tr in next ch-2 sp, ch 2) 9 times; skip 1 tr, 1 tr in each of next 2 tr, sl st to 3rd ch of first ch 5 to join.

RND 23: Ch 5, * (1 tr in next ch-2 sp, ch 2) 10 times; sk 1 tr, 1 tr in each of next 2 tr, ch 2, rep from * around. End with (1 tr in next ch-2 sp, ch 2) 10 times; sk 1 tr, 1 tr in next tr, sl st to 3rd ch of first ch 5 to join.

RND 24: Ch 5, (1 tr in next ch-2 sp, ch 2) rep between ( ) around entire doily circumference. End with sl st to 3rd ch of first ch 5 to join.

RND 25: Ch 8, * sk 2 ch-2 sps, 1 sc in next ch-2 sp, ch 5, sk 2 ch-2 sps, 5 tr in next ch-2 sp, ch 5, rep from * around. End with sk 2 ch-2 sps, 4 tr in last ch-2 sp, sl st to 3rd ch of first ch 8 to join. Fasten off.

Irish Crochet Edging (make 30 flowers in various colors)
TO START: Ch 6, join with a sl st to form ring.

RND 1: Ch 5, 1 tr in ring, ch 2, (2 tr, ch 2) 4 times into ring. End with ch 2, sl st to 3rd ch of ch 5.

RND 2: * Make 1 dc, 2 tr, 1 dc in next ch-2 sp, 1 sc in between 2 tr of previous rnd; continue with * 2 times. Make 2 tr, 12 tr in next ch-2 sp; 12 tr tr and 2 tr in next ch-2 sp. End with sl st to first petal. Turn work.

RND 3: Work back around 2 large petals only with 1 sc in each st around. Fasten off.

Attach Flowers To Doily

RND 26: Attach thread with sl st to left edge of previous 5-tr cluster, ch 6, 1 sc into previous sc, ch 6, 1 sc in 2nd tr of 5-tr cluster, ch 1, now attach flower as follows: Make 1 sc into center of 3rd smaller petal of flower, ch 1, 1 sc into 4th tr of 5-tr cluster, ch 1, 1 sc into center of first petal of smaller petals of flower, 1 sc into same 4th tr of 5-tr cluster, rep this around attaching all flowers.

FINISHING ROW: Attach same color thread as doily to beg point on first large petal of any flower. Sc into each st of 2 large petals, ch 6 across to next flower. Do not crochet around smaller petals, only the 2 large ones.

IRISH CROCHET COLLAR

Size

to fit chosen collar

Materials

1 ball (250 yards) mercerized crochet cotton, number 30

Hook

size 10

Directions

Study Figure 4-13. Make each flower as follows and then proceed to the netting.

Flower Pattern (make 5)

TO START: Ch 6, sl st to first ch to form ring.

RND 1 (top petals): Ch 3, 1 sc in ring, * ch 3, 1 sc in ring. Rep from * until 5 lps are completed. No need to sl st at end of rnd.

RND 2: In first ch-3 sp, work (1 sc, 3 hdc, 1 dc, 3 hdc, 1 sc), rep between ( ) in remaining ch-3 sps.

4-13. Irish Crochet Collar.

RND 3 (back petals): Make 1 sc in first sp (on the ch 6 that formed ring), ch 4, 1 sc in next sp (on the ch 6 that formed ring). Continue around until 4 petals are completed. Last petal work ch 4, 1 sc in first sc.

RND 4: In ch-4 sp [lp], work (1 sc, 4 hdc, 2 dc, 4 hdc, 1 sc), rep 4 times. End with sl st to first sc. Fasten off.

Work a ch the entire length of the area around each of the flowers. Secure the ch to the outside edge of each flower with tiny whip stitches through each lp.

Mesh Pattern Background

Attach thread to corner of each flower with a sl st. This sl st goes right in the ch. Ch 6, 1 sc in 6th ch that surrounds flower.

Remember that this background pat is not precise. Sometimes you need to ch 6, other times only ch 2. Attach lps with 1 dc. Follow your own judgment in placement. Pin the flower into position. Attach with 1 sc on the points of the petals as you work along with the mesh background. Work from right to left, back and forth. Fasten off. Steam press gently with medium heat.

IRISH CROCHET SNOOD

Size

approximately 15 inches in diameter

Materials

1 ball (175 yards) J. P. Coats Knit-Cro-Sheen in main color (MC)
small amounts in yellow and green or
any desired colors for pansy and leaf
round elastic
darning needle

Hook

size 5

Gauge

2 rows = 1 inch

Directions

Study Figure 4-14. Crochet the pansy, leaf, and then the snood itself (the netting). Then attach the pansy and leaf motifs to the snood.

Pansy Motif

TO START: Using yellow thread, ch 6, sl st to first ch to form ring.

RND 1: Ch 4, 2 tr in ch-6 ring; * ch 8, 3 tr in ring, rep from * until 5 ch-8 groups are worked and 5 3-tr groups are worked. End with ch 8, sl st to top of first ch 4 to join.

RND 2: Ch 4, sk 1 tr in next tr, 1 tr in next tr, * in ch-8 sp work 16 tr, 1 tr in next tr, sk 1 tr, 1 tr in next tr, rep from * around. End with sl st to first tr.

Leaf Motif

Ch to desired length of leaf; work 1 hdc in 2nd ch from hook and in each remaining ch to end; in last ch work 3 hdc; 1 hdc in each st along other side of ch; work 3 hdc in last ch. Continue working 1 hdc in each st working around leaf with 3 hdc in end hdc. Crochet your leaf as narrow or wide as you desire.

Mesh Background (Snood)

TO START: Ch 10, sl st to first ch to form ring.

RND 1: * Ch 7, 1 dc in ring, rep from * 7 times. Mark rnds with safety pin. Do not sl st at end of rnds.

RND 2: * Ch 7, 1 dc in next ch-7 sp, ch 7, 1 dc in same ch-7 sp, rep from * around.

RND 3: Ch 7, 1 dc in next ch-7 sp, * ch 7, 1 dc in next ch-7 sp, rep from * around.

RND 4 TO END: Rep Rnds 2 and 3 throughout snood. Crochet until desired size is achieved.

Assembly

When the pansy motif is complete leave 2 strings of crochet thread, each about 3 inches

4-14. Irish Crochet Snood. A snood is a hair coverlet which was worn mostly during the 1930s, 40s, and 50s. Depending upon the thread used, a snood can be made for either day or evening wear—coarser thread for the daytime and gold or silver metallic for evening.

long. This thread is used to attach leaves to pansy. After the leaves have been completed, attach the pansy by pulling 1 thread through the end of the leaf with a crochet hook. The other leaf is attached in the same manner. Tie the 2 ends tog with a knot. The leaves and pansy can now be attached to the snood with a knot. The center back of the snood is the best place for this.

Use round elastic and a darning needle to gather the outside edge of snood, with a weaving in-and-out motion. Leave enough elastic on the ends to tie in a knot. Later you can adjust the elastic to what is most comfortable for you.

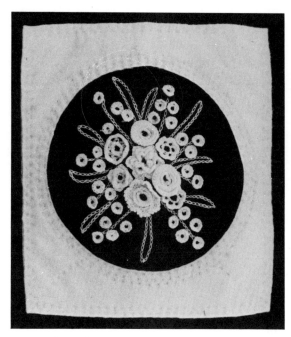

4-15. Irish Crochet Wall Hanging.

IRISH CROCHET WALL HANGING

Size

7 by 9 inches

Materials

1 ball (250 yards) mercerized crochet cotton, number 30, in white
3 pieces of felt, each 7 by 9 inches,
2 in black, 2 in white
sewing thread in white
sewing needle

Hook

size 10

Directions

Study Figure 4-15. Make each of the flowers and then assemble. (See diagram.)

Flower 1 (make 1)
TO START: Ch 8, sl st to first ch to form ring.
RND 1: Ch 2, 13 hdc in ring. End with sl st to top of first ch 2.
RND 2: 1 sc directly below and behind sl st of previous rnd on ch-8 ring; ch 8, sk 7 hdc, 1 sc at base of 7 hdc on ch-8 ring [do this from behind], ch 8, sk 7 hdc, 1 sc in first sc.
RND 3: In ch-8 sp work 12 hdc; 12 hdc in next ch-8 sp. End with sl st to first hdc.
RND 4: Make 1 sc directly below and behind sl st of previous rnd; ch 10, sk 12 hdc, 1 sc in 1 sc, ch 10. End with sl st to first sc.
RND 5: Make 16 hdc in ch-10 sp; 16 hdc in next ch-10 sp. End with sl st to first hdc.
RND 6: Make 1 sc at bottom of sl st, ch 3, sk 4 hdc, 1 sc at base of hdc [from behind], * ch 3, sk 4 hdc, rep from * until 6 ch-3 lps are worked. End with sl st to base of first ch 3.
RND 7: * In ch-3 sp, work (1 sc, 3 hdc, 1 sc), rep from * around until all 6 ch-3 sps are complete. End with sl st to first ch 3.
RND 8: * Make 1 sc in 1 sc, ch 2, 1 sc in 1 hdc, ch 2, 1 sc in 1 hdc, ch 2, 1 sc in 1 hdc, ch 2, 1 sc in 1 sc, rep from * around. End with sl st to first sc. Fasten off.

Flower 2 (make 2)
Work the same as for flower 1 up to Rnd 5.
RND 6: Make 1 sc in each of 32 hdc around. End with sl st to first sc. Fasten off.

Flower 3 (make 1)
TO START: Ch 6, sl st to first ch to form ring.
RND 1: Ch 5, 1 sc in ring, * ch 5, 1 sc in ring, rep from * until 6 petals are worked. End with sl st to base of first ch 5.
RND 2: (1 sc, 2 hdc, 1 dc, 2 hdc, 1 sc) in each

ch-5 sp around. End with sl st to first sc.

RND 3: Ch 1, 1 sc in middle of first ch 5 [on the ch 6 that formed ring], ch 5, 1 sc in middle of next ch 5. Continue around until 6 petals are formed. End with ch 5 and sl st to first sc.

RND 4: * (1 sc, 2 hdc, 2 dc, 2 hdc, 1 sc) in first ch 5. Rep from * in each ch-5 sp. End with sl st to first sc.

RND 5: Ch 1, 1 sc behind and between first and 2nd petals, * ch 5, 1 sc between next petal, rep from * until 6 petals are formed. End with sl st to first ch 1.

RND 6: (1 sc, 3 hdc, 2 hdc, 3 hdc, 1 sc) in each petal around. End with sl st to first sc. Fasten off.

Flower 4 (make 1)

TO START: Ch 8, sl st to first ch to form ring.

RND 1: Ch 2, 13 hdc in ring. End with sl st to top of ch 2.

RND 2: * Ch 4, sk 1 hdc, 1 sc in next hdc directly below and behind on ch 8 (ch 8 that formed ring). Rep from * until 7 ch-4s are complete. End with ch 4, 1 sc in base of first ch 4.

RND 3: Sl st up 2 chs of ch 4, * 1 sc in next ch-4 sp, ch 4, rep from * around. End with ch 4, sl st to base of first ch 4.

RND 4: Ch 2, (2 hdc, 2 dc, 3 hdc) in ch-4 sp, * (3 hdc, 2 dc, 3 hdc) in next ch-4 sp, rep from * around. End with sl st to first ch 2. Fasten off.

Flower 5 (make 2)

TO START: Ch 6, sl st to first ch to form ring.

RND 1: Ch 5, 1 sc in ring; rep until 6 ch-5s are complete. Do not sl st at end of rnd.

RND 2: * (1 sc, 3 hdc, 2 dc, 3 hdc, 1 sc) in first ch-5 sp, rep from * in remaining ch-5 sps. Fasten off.

Flower 6 (make 1)

Follow Flower 3, except making only 4 rnds.

Buds (make 30)

TO START: Ch 4, sl st to first ch to form ring.

RND 1: Ch 2, 10 hdc in ring. End with sl st to top of ch 2. Fasten off.

Assembling

See Figure 4-16. After all flowers are made they are now ready to be attached to the felt picture frame. Arrange the flowers as shown in the diagram. Secure with pins. They are all attached by tacking them to the background. The leaves on the outside of the main design are done with a ch st.

Felt pieces are put tog as shown in the diagram. They are held tog by outlining the felt with a simple running stitch done by hand. [They can also be done by sewing machine.] The outside has 2 rows of hand stitching. The outside of the circle has 3 rows. The areas from the corners to the circle are done with 1 line of hand stitching.

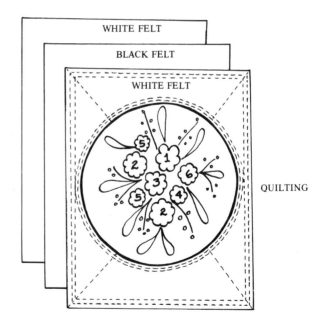

QUILTING

4-16. Assembling the wall hanging.

79

4-17. Irish Crochet Pincushion.

IRISH CROCHET PINCUSHION

Size
4½ inches wide by 3 inches long

Materials
small amount of mercerized crochet cotton, number 30
¼ yard muslin
sewing thread to match muslin
sewing needle

Hook
size 10

Directions
Study Figure 4-17. The first step is to construct the pincushion and crochet the ruffle around it. Then crochet the flowers and the netting. The netting is crocheted into the pincushion's ruffle and is used to anchor the flowers in place.

Pincushion
Trace a heart shape and cut out the pattern. Transfer the heart shape to material, pin, and cut out 2 pieces. Heart can be either machine-stitched or hand-sewn. Leave an opening for turning to the right side.

Fill pincushion with any number of things, such as old, dried coffee grounds, sawdust, white beach sand, or cornstarch. Once heart is filled, sew opening with whip stitches to close.

Ruffle
Sc around entire edge of heart, working through both pieces of material. Keep sc sts close together. End with sl st to first sc.
RND 1: Ch 2, 1 dc in each sc around heart. End with sl st to top of first dc.
RND 2: Ch 3, 3 tr in each dc around heart to give ruffle effect. End with sl st to top of first ch 3. Fasten off.

Flower Motif (make 4)
TO START: Ch 5, sl st to first ch to form ring.
RND 1: * Ch 4, 1 sc in ring, rep from * until 6 petals are worked. No need to sl st at end.
RND 2: (1 sc, 5 tr, 1 sc) in each ch-4 sp around. End with sl st to first sc to join.

Background Netting
This netting has no precise pat. Sl st thread in 1 dc on parameter of heart; * ch 6, sk 5 dc, 1 dc in next st, rep from * around heart. Continue around heart and as you work closer to motifs, attach petals with 1 sc.

IRISH CROCHET ROSE CHOKER

Size
1½ inches in diameter

Materials
small amounts of mercerized crochet cotton, number 20, in white, pink, red, or ecru for the rose, and green for the leaves

Hook
size 5

Directions
Study Figure 4-18. Start out by making the rose, then the leaves, and then the ch.

Rose
TO START: Ch 6, sl st to first ch to form ring.
RND 1: * Ch 4, 1 sc in ring, rep from * until 5 ch-4's are completed. No need to sl st at end of rnd.
RND 2: In first ch 4, work (1 sc, 3 hdc, 1 sc), rep between ( ) in each ch-4 sp around. End with sl st to first sc.
RND 3: Ch 1, from behind 1 sc in ch-4 sp on ch 6 that formed the ring; * ch 5, from behind 1 sc in ch-4 sp on ch 6 that formed the ring; rep from * around. End with ch 5, sl st to first ch 1.
RND 4: In first ch-5 sp work (1 sc, 5 hdc, 1 sc), rep between ( ) in each ch-5 sp around. End with sl st to first sc.
RND 5: Rep Rnd 3, except ch 6.
RND 6: Rep Rnd 4 except work (1 sc, 5 hdc, 4 dc, 5 hdc, 1 sc) in each ch-6 sp around.
RND 7: Rep Rnd 3, except ch 7.
RND 8: Rep Rnd 4, except work (1 sc, 5 hdc, 5 dc, 5 hdc, 1 sc). End with sl st in first sc.
Continue around with 1 sc in each st around. End with sl st to first sc.
Starting at Rnd 2, make 1 sc in each stitch around. Fasten off.

4-18. Irish Crochet Rose Choker.

Leaf
TO START: Ch 5, sl st to first ch to form ring.
RND 1: Ch 2, work 13 hdc in ring. End with sl st to top of ch 2.
RND 2: Ch 2, work 2 hdc in each hdc around. End with sl st to top of first ch 2.
RND 3: Ch 2, 1 dc in each of next 7 hdc, * (ch 2, turn work, 1 dc in each of next 8 dc) rep between ( ) 3 times; ch 1, turn work, 1 sc in each of next 8 dc. Fasten off.
On the opposite side of rose, just opposite leaf completed, work another leaf using the above instructions. Attach thread with sl st and ch 2, work 1 dc in each of next 7 hdc, follow directions given from * in above directions.

Chain for Rose Choker
With crochet hook work as many ch sts as required to go comfortably around the neck. Fasten end and cut off.

C H A P T E R   F I V E

INSERTIONS

A beautiful way to give blouses, aprons, lingerie, and linens a delicate "old-fashioned" look is to insert crocheted motifs or filet designs.

Insertions are simply crocheted pieces done separately and then attached to the fabric. The difference between an insertion and a trim, or border (see Chapter 6), can be seen clearly in Figure 5-1. With an insertion, the fabric is cut away and the crocheted piece is attached within the open space. A trim, or border, on the other hand, is attached to an edge of the fabric. In the photograph, the square panel of filet crochet is an insert and the motifs at the bottom edge are border, or trim.

5-1. A linen hand towel with a filet-crocheted letter B as an insertion and a motif trim attached at the edge. The towel belonged to the John Bergman Family. From the collection of Helen Svinicki. (See page 83.)

APPLYING INSERTIONS

Place the crocheted piece to be inserted on top of the fabric in the exact position you want. Pin and then baste it in place. Leaving a ¼-inch seam allowance for a hem all around, cut the fabric now covered by the insertion away so that the insertion will fill the space. Fold the fabric back and hand-stitch a narrow hem on the fabric opening using a whip stitch.

INSERTIONS WITH RIBBONS

Ribbon insertions are decorative additions to camisoles, curtains, and aprons. Figure 5-2 shows a good example of this technique ap-

plied. However, in this case, the ribbon is technically a trim, rather than an insertion. Figure 2-2 is another good example of ribbon insertion. Open spaces are worked into an openwork filet-type crocheted piece and then ribbon, often velvet, is weaved in and out of the spaces. (See diagram.) To make the holes through which you will weave:

Work 1 dc in st of previous row, ch 1, sk 1 st, rep across, Ch 3, turn. Work next row with pat st desired, crocheting 1 st over the skipped st.

If you desire larger spaces for holes to accommodate wider ribbon, substitute treble crochet for the double crochet in directions above.

5-3. Applying ribbon insertions.

5-2. A ribbon insertion used as ties for an apron.

ROUND TABLECLOTH
WITH DOILY INSERT

Size

60 inches in diameter

Materials

6 balls (450 yards each) mercerized crochet cotton, number 20
suitable fabric for tablecloth, 60 inches in diameter (if you use a sheet, there will be no center seam)
sewing thread to match
sewing needle

Hook

size 10

Gauge

3 shells = 1 inch
5 rows = 1 inch

Directions

Study Figures 5-4, 5-5, 5-6, and 5-7. The tablecloth consists of a doily insertion, a lace insertion that surrounds the doily, and a lace edging.

Doily Insertion
TO START: Ch 7, sl st to form ring.
RND 1: Ch 3, 23 dc in ring. End with sl st to top of first ch 3.
RND 2: Ch 5, 1 dc in same place as sl st, ch 2, * sk 3 dc, 1 dc between 3rd and 4th dc, ch 3, 1 dc in same place [V made], ch 2, rep from * until 8 Vs are made. End with sl st to top of first ch 3.
RND 3: Ch 3, 4 tr in V sp, * ch 1, 5 tr in next V sp, rep from * around. End with ch 2, sl st to top of first ch 3.
RND 4: Ch 3, turn; 1 dc in ch-2 sp; * ch 2, 1 dc in

5-4. Round Tablecloth With Doily Insertion.

3rd dc, ch 3, 1 dc in same dc [V made]; ch 2, 1 dc in ch-1 sp, ch 3, 1 dc in same sp [V made]; rep from * around. End with ch 2, sl st to top of first ch 3.
RND 5: Rep Rnd 3.
RND 6: Rep Rnd 4.
RND 7: Rep Rnd 3 except do not ch 1 between 5 tr.
RND 8: Ch 6, * 1 sc between 5 tr, ch 6, rep from * around. End with sl st to base of first ch 6.
RND 9: Ch 3, 4 tr in ch-6 sp, * ch 3, 1 sc in next ch-6 sp, ch 3, 5 tr in next ch-6 sp, rep from * around. End with sl st to top of first ch 3.
RND 10: Ch 6, * 1 sc in ch-3 sp, ch 6, 1 sc in next ch-3 sp, ch 6, rep from * around. End with sl st to top of first ch 6.
RND 11: Ch 3, 5 tr in ch-6 sp, * ch 3, 1 sc in next

5-5. Detail of doily and lace insertion.

ch-6 sp, ch 3, 6 tr in next ch-6 sp, rep from * around. End with ch 3, sl st to top of first ch 3.

RND 12: * Ch 6, 1 sc in ch-3 sp, ch 6, 1 sc in next ch-3 sp, rep from * around. End with sl st to top of first ch 6.

RND 13: (Ch 3, 3 tr, ch 2, 4 tr) in ch-6 sp [1st shell made]; * ch 2, 1 sc in next ch-6 sp; ch 2, (4 tr, ch 2, 4 tr) in next ch-6 sp [another shell]; rep from * around. End with sl st to top of first ch 3.

RND 14: Sl st up to ch-2 sp, (ch 3, 3 tr, ch 2, 4 tr) in ch-2 sp [shell made]; * ch 2, 1 sc in sc, ch 2, (4 tr, ch 2, 4 tr) in next ch-2 sp of previous shell [another shell]; rep from * around. End with ch 2, sl st to top of first ch 3.

RND 15: Sl st up to ch-2 sp, * ch 6, 1 sc in next sc, ch 6, 1 sc in ch-2 sp, rep from * around. End with ch 6, sl st to first ch-2 sp.

RND 16: Rep Rnd 15 except ch 7.

RND 17: Rep Rnd 16.

RND 18: Ch 3, turn, 10 sc in ch-7 sp, * ch 3, 10 sc in next ch-7 sp, rep from * around.

RND 19: Ch 3, turn, 4 tr in ch-3 sp, * ch 3, 5 tr in next ch-3 sp, rep from * around. End with ch 3, sl st to top of first ch 3.

RND 20: Sl st up to 3rd tr; * ch 7, 1 sc in 3rd tr of next 5 tr, rep from * around.

RND 21: Ch 3, 9 tr in ch-7 sp, * 10 tr in next ch-7 sp, rep from * around. Fasten off.

Lace Edging

TO START: Ch 25, beginning in 5th ch from hook, work 1 dc, ch 3, 1 dc in same ch [V made]. * Ch 2, sk 3 ch, 1 dc in next ch, ch 3, 1 dc in same ch, rep from * until 5 V's are crocheted. End with ch 2, sk 3 ch and 1 dc in next ch, ch 3, turn.

ROW 2: Make 5 tr in first V, * ch 1, 5 tr in next V, rep from * until end. End with ch 2, 1 dc in ch-3 sp, ch 3, turn.

ROW 3: * Make 1 dc in 3rd tr, ch 3, 1 dc in same place, ch 2, rep from * to end.

Rep Rows 2 and 3 until desired length of the lace is complete, do not break off thread. End with 5 tr, ch 3, * 1 sc in ch-3 sp, 5 tr in ch-3 sp, rep from * across entire length of bottom of lace. Fasten off.

Lace Insertion

Crochet lace following directions for Lace Edging, except ch 17 to start. Continue crocheting lace until the length is long enough to make a circle around the Doily Insertion. In order to get the roundness needed, attach thread with sc to corner of lace, * ch 4, 1 sc in ch-3 sp (next to 5 trs), ch 4, 1 sc in next ch-3 sp, rep from * to the end of the lace. This will give the lace a fan effect and the needed circular shape.

5-6. Detail of lace trim for Round Tablecloth.

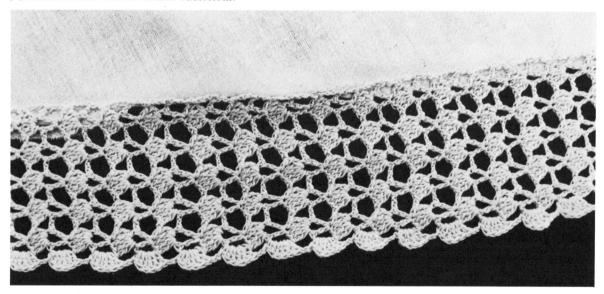

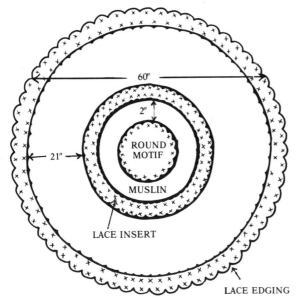

5-7. Assembling the tablecloth.

Assembling

Cut a 57-inch circle from fabric. Carefully machine-stitch a narrow edge around entire circumference of fabric circle, avoiding pulling. Whip-stitch ends of lace together. Lay lace insert into place as shown in diagram. Pin and baste in place. Cut away fabric from insert, leaving a ½-inch allowance for hems. Remove basting and hem cut away portion with a narrow machine hem. Check the width of opening with width of lace so that insert will fit. Pin and baste doily motif in center of cloth. Cut away fabric from insert, leaving a ½-inch allowance for hem. Remove basting and hem cut away portion with a narrow machine hem. Repin and baste inserts into place in openings and carefully machine stitch into place.

NOTE: Use small basting stitches to prevent pulling when machine stitching.

88

APRON WITH FILET-RADISH INSERT

Size
5 by 10 inches

Materials
1 ball (200 yards) mercerized crochet cotton, number 10
1½ yards calico print fabric, 44/45 inch wide
sewing thread to match
sewing needle

Hook
size 7

Gauge
10 dc = 1 inch
9 rows = 1 inch

Directions
Study Figure 5-8. Make the insert first and then assemble the apron as directed. Follow the filet crochet instructions in Chapter 3.

Filet-Radish Insert
TO START: Ch 44. Dc in 6th ch from hook. *Ch 1, sk 1 ch, 1 dc in next ch, rep from * to end of ch. End with ch 6 and turn. Work back across with 1 dc in each st across. From this point follow graph row by row. Use a ch 6 at end of each row for turning ch and dc in 3rd ch of ch 6 to keep work square.

Assembling
Cut the following pieces from the calico fabric:
Bib—two 10½ by 13½ inches
Ties—two 27 by 3 inches
Neck Strap—one 20 by 3 inches
Skirt—one 18 by 30 inches
Bottom Ruffle—one 6 by 44 inches
    Apply Radish Insert to one of Bib pieces as

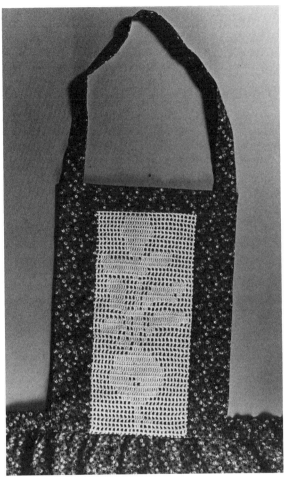

5-8. Apron With Filet-Radish Insertion. Filet insert designed by Karla Thompson. Apron designed and made by Chris Ruleau.

follows: Place the radish crocheted piece on the fabric so that a border is formed on the sides and top, and the bottom of the radish piece should align evenly with the bottom of the bib. Pin and baste in place. Cut material out so that insert will fill the space, leaving a ¼-inch allowance all around the fabric for a hem. Stitch a narrow hem on the fabric opening, then stitch the crocheted insertion into place using a whip stitch.

Using ½-inch seams, sew long, raw edges of Neck Strap together, leaving ends open. Turn right side out and press flat. Make Ties in a similar fashion, sewing one end of each closed and leaving 6 inches open on opposite long edge. Pin right sides of bib tog with ends of neck strap pinned in place on top of bib and ties pinned ½ inch up from bottom edge, seams down. With ½-inch seams, sew around, starting above opening for tie, leaving ties pinned in place, through. Leave bottom of bib open. Turn right side out and press.

Stitch a narrow rolled hem on 1 long side and both ends of bottom ruffle. Run gathering stitches on other long side. Sew narrow rolled hem on sides of skirt. Attach ruffle to skirt bottom, adjusting gathers to fit. Gather top of skirt. Pin skirt to bib, extending skirt into open seam that has been left open in the tie. Press all seams up into bib and tie. Edge st. Tie in place 1 bib bottom. Edge st the open seam of tie.

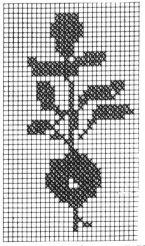

5-9. Graph for Radish. START

5-10. Flower Basket With Ribbon Insertion.

FLOWER BASKET WITH RIBBON INSERT

Size

9 inches wide, 8 inches tall (including handle)

Materials

1 ball (200 yards) mercerized crochet cotton, number 10
1 yard grosgrain ribbon, ⅜ inch wide
laundry starch

Hook

size 3

Directions

Study Figure 5-10. Make the basket, ruffle, and handle, starch the basket, and then weave the ribbon in the sps worked into the crochet.

Body of Basket

TO START: Ch 8, join with sl st to form ring.
RND 1: Make 13 sc in ring, join with sl st to first st.
RND 2: Make 1 dc in each sc around, inc 6 dc evenly around. End with sl st to first st.
RND 3: Make 1 dc in each dc around, inc 11 dc evenly around. End with sl st to first st.
RND 4: Make 1 dc in each dc around, inc 16 dc evenly around. End with sl st to first st.
RND 5: Make 2 tr in each of next 3 dc, 2 dc in each of next 2 dc, * 1 sc in each of next 13 dc and at the same time also inc 4 sc evenly spaced 2 sc in each of next 2 dc, 2 tr in each of next 3 dc, 2 dc in each of next 2 dc, 1 sc in each dc across to last 2 dc, and at the same time also inc 2 sc evenly spaced; work 2 dc in each of next 2 dc. This forms oval base of basket.
RND 6: Make 1 dc in each st around, inc 14 sts evenly spaced. End with sl st to first st.
RNDS 7–10: Make 1 dc in each st around. End with sl st to first st.

RND 11: Make 1 dc in each st around, inc 7 sts evenly spaced. End with sl st to first st.
RND 12: Make 1 tr in each dc around. End with sl st to first st.
RND 13: (spacing for ribbon insertion): * Make 1 dc in next st, ch 3, sk 1 st, rep from * around. End with sl st to first st.
RND 14: Make 1 dc in each st around. End with sl st to first st.
RND 15: * Ch 3, sk 1 st, 1 sc in next st, rep from * around. End with sl st to first st.
RNDS 16–18: Ch 6, * 1 dc in center of previous ch-3 sp, ch 6, rep from * around. End off on Rnd 18.

Bottom Ruffle

At any point on edge of Rnd 6, attach thread and work 1 dc in each st around Rnd 6, increasing as necessary to keep row flat.
RND 2: * Ch 3, sk 1 st, 1 sc in next st, rep from * around. End off.

Handle

Attach thread to Rnd 13 on center point of long side of oval. Work 8 dc into Rnd 13, ch 2, turn work. Work 1 dc into each dc, ch 2, turn work for 5 rows. On next row, dec 1 st on each side and work the handle with 6 dc for 9 inches. Inc 1 st on each side and work the handle with 8 dc for 3 more rows. Attach handle to opposite side of basket with sc. Fasten off.

Finishing

Starch the basket extra heavily. Follow the directions on the package for boiled starch and make sure the basket is thoroughly saturated with starch. Do not squeeze out too much of the excess starch. As the basket begins to dry, shape it into an oval shape with the ruffle extending and handle upright. Allow the basket to dry thoroughly. Weave ribbon and tie bow.

5-11. Curtains With
Filet-Rose Panels.

CURTAINS WITH FILET-ROSE PANELS

Size

The amounts listed below are based on a curtain measuring 4 feet in length, but you can make your curtain to fit any size window.

Materials

8 balls (400 yards each) mercerized crochet cotton, number 50
1¾ yards percale fabric
sewing thread to match
sewing needle

Hook

size 13

Gauge

16 dc = 1 inch
5 rows = 1 inch

Directions

Study Figure 5-11. Each filet-crocheted panel is sewn to a fabric panel. Then the filet-crocheted valance is added to the top. Follow the instructions in Chapter 3 for filet crochet.

Filet-Rose Panels
TO START: Ch 90. Dc in 6th ch from hook. Continue following graph row by row, working filled sps with 2 dc instead of the usual 1 dc and work 2 chs instead of the usual 1 ch in open sps. Continue to the 28 rows of the graph until desired length of panel is achieved. For a window about 30 inches wide, crochet 3 panels.
TO FINISH: Dc around entire edge of each panel, working 2 dc in each sp. Then work a picot edge into dc edge as follows: * Ch 2, sk 2 dc, make 1 dc in next dc, (ch 6, sl st into first ch of ch 6) [picot formed], rep from * around. Fasten off.

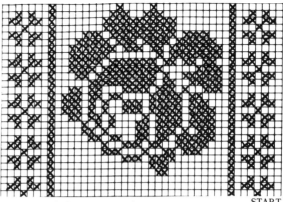

5-12. Graph for Rose panel.   START

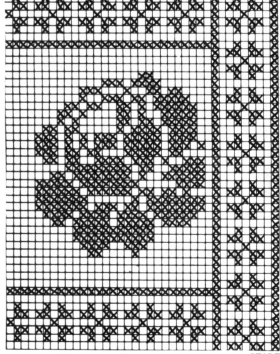

5-13. Graph for Rose valance.   START

Rose Valance
Valance should be 3 or 4 inches wider than the actual measurement of window to allow for a

slight fullness. Each rose motif of the valance measures approximately 4½ inches in width. From this, count how many rose motifs you will need for your valance adding 3 inches for the end borders. The sample valance (see photograph) has 6 rose motifs.

Count the number of squares in the graph (Figure 5-13) from spaces 10 to 35 and multiply that figure by the number of motifs you will need for your own particular window. Add to this number the 2 end borders which number 9 each end. Multiply the total figure times 2 plus add 6 for turning. This final figure is the number you will need to ch to begin the valance.

$$
\begin{aligned}
&\ 26 \text{ spaces per rose motif}\\
&\underline{\times\ \ \ \ 6 \text{ (total number of motifs needed)}}\\
&= 156\\
&\underline{+\ \ 18 \text{ number of spaces of 2 end borders}}\\
&= 174 \text{ number of spaces for valance}\\
&\underline{\times\ \ \ \ 2}\\
&\ \ 348\\
&\underline{+\ \ \ \ 6 \text{ for turning}}\\
&= 354 \text{ total number of chains needed to begin}\\
& \text{valance}
\end{aligned}
$$

TO START: Ch 354. Dc in 6th ch from hook. Continue, following graph row by row, working filled sps with 2 dc and open sps with 2 chs. When finished, dc around entire edges of each panel and valance. Work 2 dc in each sp. Work a picot edge into dc edge as follows: * Ch 2, sk 2 dc, make 1 dc in next dc, (ch 6, sl st into first ch of ch 6) [picot formed], rep from * around. Fasten off.

Assembling
For a 3-panel rose curtain which will fit a window approximately 30 inches wide, cut 4 lengths of fabric each 10 to 12 inches wide. [Allow approximately twice the fullness of your window for your total curtain width.] The length of the fabric should be the same as your panels. Hem each fabric panel edge by machine or by hand. Carefully baste the crocheted rose panels to the fabric panels, then hand-stitch into place with whip stitches. Machine stitching can be done, but is not as desirable because it tends to pull the fabric. Zigzag across bottom of curtain. Cut a 6-inch piece of fabric which will be as long as the curtain width. Make a rod pocket from this piece for the top of the curtain. Run a gathering stitch across top of rod pocket and pull to width needed to fit your window. Then hand-stitch the valance to the gathered rod pocket at top of curtain. Make a fabric ruffle for the bottom or turn up and hem by hand.

PILLOW WITH FILET-TULIPS INSERT

Size
13 by 13 inches

Materials
1 ball (250 yards) mercerized crochet cotton, number 30
½ yard rose print fabric
½ yard rose-colored fabric
sewing thread to match
sewing needle

Hook
size 7

Gauge
11 dc = 1 inch
7 rows = 1 inch

5-14. Pillow With Filet-Tulips Insertion.

Directions

Study Figure 5-15. Crochet the filet rose design, then make the lace edging ruffle and assemble the pillow as directed. Follow the filet crochet instructions in Chapter 3.

Filet-Tulips Insert

TO START: Ch 57. Establish a foundation row by working as follows: Beginning in 6th ch from hook, work 1 dc, *ch 1, work 1 dc, rep from * across to end of ch. Now follow graph

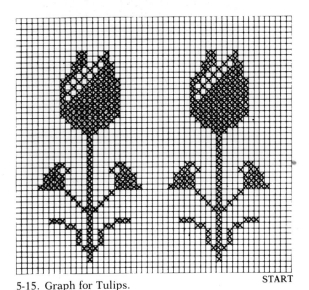

5-15. Graph for Tulips.   START

back and forth, filling in sps with 1 dc where indicated with an x. Ch 4 and tr turn at the end of each row. Work piece until it measures approximately 8½ by 8½ inches. Fasten off.

Lace Edging Ruffle

TO START: Ch enough sts to measure 4 feet.
ROW 1: Working in 4th ch from hook, dc in next ch, *sk 1 st, ch 1, dc in next ch, rep from * across to end of ch, ch 5, turn work.
ROW 2: Work 1 dc in 2nd dc from hook, *work 2 dc in sp, [1 inc made], work 1 dc in next dc, rep from * across, ch 5, turn.
ROW 3: Work 1 dc in 2nd dc from hook, * ch 1, sk 1 dc, dc in next dc, rep from * across, ch 5, turn.
ROW 4 (picot edge): Work 1 dc in 2nd dc from hook, *ch 3, work 3 sc in sp, work 1 dc in next dc, rep from * across, fasten off.

Assembling

To make the rose border cut a square from the rose-colored fabric to measure 13½ by 13½

inches. Fold under 1¼ inches on each edge of fabric, then fold another 1¼ inches. A 1¼-inch border will have been made. Hand-stitch into place overlapping slightly the fabric edge and crocheted edge.

To make the print border cut 4 strips of flower print fabric, each 2½ inches wide, 12½ inches long. Fold and press under ½ inch on each edge, then fold and press under again. Stitch this flowered border to the edge of rose-colored border. Turn under corner edges and stitch.

To make the ruffle cut 8 feet of flower print, 4½ inches wide. Piece where necessary. Fold strip in half lengthwise, with wrong sides tog. Run a gathering st ¼ inch from raw edge of folded strip. Gather to fit around pillow.

Cut a rose-colored square for back of pillow, ¾ inch larger than front square. Fold and press under ¾ inch of back square. Lay ruffle in between back and front and stitch into place, leaving an opening for stuffing. Stuff pillow with polyester stuffing, and hand-stitch the opening. Lastly hand-stitch crocheted lace edging ruffle into place.

GUEST TOWELS WITH FILET INSERT

Size

12 by 16½ inches

Materials

1 ball (250 yards) mercerized crochet cotton, number 30
1 yard huck toweling
sewing thread to match
sewing needle

96

Hook

size 10

Gauge

7 rows = 1 inch

Directions

Study Figure 5-17. Follow the directions for assembling the towels after you have crocheted the filet design.

Filet Insert

TO START: Ch 32. Dc in 6th ch from hook, *ch 1, sk 1 ch, and dc in next. Rep from * until the end of the ch. Continue row by row, following the graph, working the filled-in sps in double

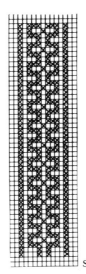

START

5-17. Graph for filet design.

5-16. Guest Towels With Filet Insertion.

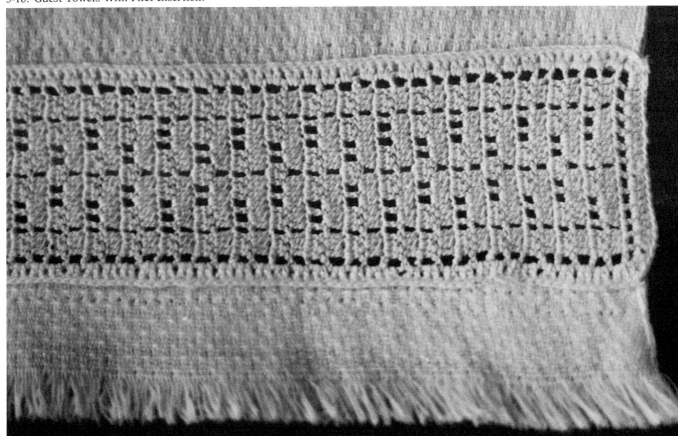

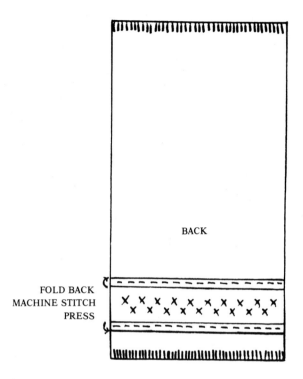

BACK

FOLD BACK
MACHINE STITCH
PRESS

5-18. Assembling the guest towel.

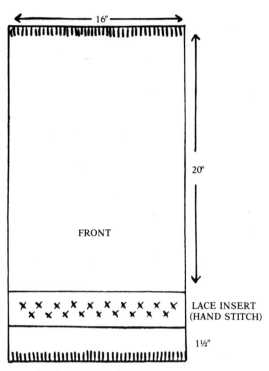

16″

20″

FRONT

LACE INSERT
(HAND STITCH)

1½″

PULL THREADS (FRINGE)

mesh crochet. [Please read directions on page 54 for double mesh crochet.] Be sure to keep sides of lace even and ending squares even also. This can be accomplished by always chaining 6 to turn and ending the rows with a dc in 3rd ch of ch 6. Rep geometric design as many times as necessary for the desired length.

When finished, read instructions at the beg of Chapter 3 on how to block, and block the lace.

Assembling
See Figure 5-18. At the short end of the towel measure up 2 inches. From the main piece of huck towel fold fabric back ½ inch and press with iron. Take the small strip of fabric and fold back ½ inch also. Press. Machine-sew the crochet geometric design to the bottom of main piece of huck towel. Guide fabric and crochet design carefully. Do not stretch. When this is completed, sew other edge of crochet design to small strip of fabric as previously described. The ends of the towel can either be fringed or folded back ¼ inch and sewn. If towel is fringed, the fringe is approximately ½ inch. Press entire towel with steam iron.

TABLE RUNNER WITH FILET INSERT

Size

13 by 46 inches

Materials

3 balls (250 yards each) mercerized crochet cotton, number 30
1 yard muslin fabric, 36 inches wide
sewing thread to match
sewing needle

Hook

size 10

Gauge

6 rows = 1 inch

Directions

Study Figure 5-20. After you have crocheted the insert and edging, follow the directions for assembling the runner.

5-19. Table Runner With Filet Insertion.

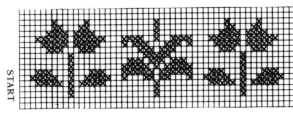

START

5-20. Graph for filet edging.

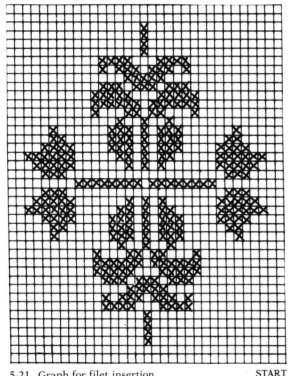

5-21. Graph for filet insertion.   START

Filet Edging

TO START: Ch 42. Dc in 6th ch from hook, * ch 1, sk 1 ch, and dc in next, rep from * until the end of ch. Continue row by row, following the graph, the filled-in sps in double mesh crochet. [Please see instructions on page 54 for double mesh crochet.] Be sure to keep sides of lace even and ending squares even also. This can be accomplished by always chaining 6 to turn and ending the row with a dc in 3rd ch of chain 6. Rep pat of tulips and iris for the desired length. Make 2 pieces of lace each 2¾ by 46 inches. When finished, read blocking instructions on page 19, and block the piece.

Filet Insert

TO START: Ch 72, and proceed with insert as with Edging.

Assembly

See Figure 5-22. Cut out a piece of muslin fabric 9 by 46 inches. Fold long sides over twice, ½ inch once and then again ½ inch. Rep with other side. Press into place with steam iron. Attach filet lace to edge either by hand sewing with the whip stitch or with sewing machine. Do not stretch. Sew close to lace edge, but sew about ½ inch into body of fabric on folded edge. After completion, press with steam iron.

Pin filet crochet insert in the middle of fabric piece. Turn fabric over. On this wrong side cut out material that covers the insertion. Cut to within ½ inch of edge. Fold ½ inch of fabric to the outside of the insertion. [Corners will have to be cut.] Do this by cutting at an angle. Secure the insertion with an overcasted stitch on the back of the fabric. Press this after completion.

RUNNER

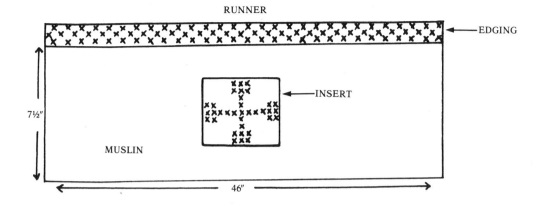

EDGING

INSERT

7½″

MUSLIN

46″

DETAIL OF INSERT

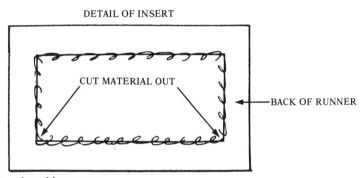

CUT MATERIAL OUT

BACK OF RUNNER

5-22. Assembling the table runner.

C H A P T E R S I X

TRIMS

The old crochet instruction booklets were filled with directions for fancy trims of all sorts. Borders, edgings, and laces were added to many household linens, such as quilts, blankets, towels, sheets, and pillowcases, and, of course, handkerchiefs (see Figure 6-1.) Most laces and edgings were worked with a fine hook and thread so that the result would be much like a machine lace. Within this chapter are instructions for a variety of edgings. Some are as simple as the picot and shell edging. Seek out some of the old crochet books or take a look at some of the books listed in the Bibliography. Then, as the ladies did years ago, trim your aprons, shawls, and household linens with your crochet work. See Figures 6-2 through 6-11 for some inspirations.

6-1. Fancy edgings for hankies. From the collection of Cheryl Harris. (See page 103.)

6-2. This linen handkerchief with a wide border of Irish crochet belonged to Mrs. William F. Shirley of New York City in the late 19th century. Reproduced with permission of the Smithsonian Institute.

6-3. A linen doily with a cotton scalloped edging. From the collection of Eunice Svinicki.

6-4. A 10-inch-wide border for a church vestment made by Tina Bergman.

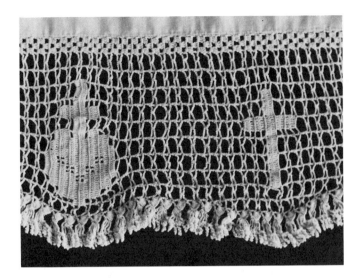

6-5. An ecru edging around a linen doily. Note the row of single crochet around the doily around which the edging is worked.

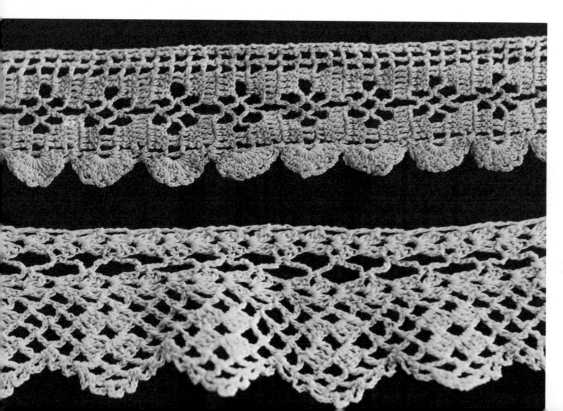

6-8. Scalloped cotton edgings made by Tina Bergman.

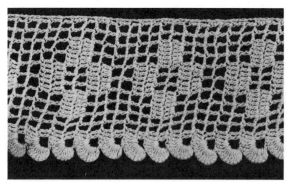

6-9. Filet crochet lace with scalloped edging by Tina Bergman.

6-11. A border of motifs.

6-10. An 8-inch-wide cotton lace border. From the collection of Eunice Svinicki.

MAKING EDGINGS

Edgings can be used to trim such items as hankies, doilies, pillows, pillowcases, and wearing apparel; and crocheted items themselves, such as doilies, tablecloths, and shawls, are often beautifully enhanced by the addition of the right edging. To crochet an edging around a fabric piece, such as a fabric doily, first you must machine- or hand-stitch a narrow hem on the fabric to be trimmed. The next step is to make a base of single crochet stitches around the entire hem. Attach the crochet thread to any side with a slip stitch, then begin to place single crochet stitches into the fabric just at the top of the hem. Use one stitch for every machine stitch in the hem, or about five per ½ inch. Use two or three stitches in each corner so that the corners will not pull. To end, slip stitch to the first stitch. This base forms a sturdy, yet neat, foundation for the edging. After completing this single crochet base, you can follow the directions for the particular edging you desire.

Attaching an edging to a crochet piece is quite simple, and directions for three popular edgings follow.

Picot Edging

One of the most popular edge finishes is the picot edging (see Figure 6-12), and hundreds of variations on the picot edging are possible. The following are directions for one of the most simple of picot edgings:

Join the thread at side edge of the crocheted piece you want to trim with a sl st. * Ch 4, work 1 sc into 4th ch from hook. This forms 1 picot. Work 1 sc in each of next 4 sts. Rep from * across.

The distance between the picots can vary and also the number of chs in the picot can be increased. Work this edging onto fabric or into the final row of a crocheted piece.

6-12. Basic Picot Edging.

Shell Edging

The shell edging (see Figure 6-13) is another popular trim. Sometimes the shell edging can be used in combination with picots for a fancier finish. Once you know the technique for both, you can experiment for yourself.

Join the thread at the side edge with a sl st.
ROW 1: *Work 1 dc in next st, ch 1, sk 1 st, rep from * across. End with ch 4, turn work.
ROW 2: Work a dc in first ch-1 sp of previous row, ch 1, (* work 1 dc, ch 1 into next ch-1 sp of previous row) rep between ( ) 4 times; sk 1 ch-1 sp, rep from * across.

Popcorn Edging

The popcorn edging (see Figure 6-14) is more dimensional than various other types of edgings. Because of its bumpiness and distinct look, the popcorn edging lends itself to curtain edgings, sweaters, and almost anything that needs an extra special look.

ROW 1: Sc in first 4 sts along edge row, * ch 3, work 5 dc into 3rd ch just worked [1 popcorn made], remove hook and insert into top of ch 3, sl st through dropped st, ch 1, sc into base of popcorn, sc in next 4 sts, rep from * across.

6-13. Basic Shell Edging.

MAKING TASSELS

Tassels were first used primarily for pulls on window shades. They were seen as edgings for piano covers, as curtains, and archways were usually adorned with fringes attached to fancy crochet work. Nightcaps too had tassels, as did baby caps and evening bags.

Small Tassel

To make a small tassel cut a piece of cardboard 2 inches square and wind the thread around the cardboard approximately fifty times. (See diagram.) Cut another 5-inch length of thread and pass it through one folded end. (See diagram.) Tie its ends together and slip the other folded end of the wound thread with scissors. Remove the cardboard. With another length of thread wrap a few turns all around the tied end, about ½ inch from end. Secure ends and hide inside the tassel. Trim tassel ends evenly.

Large Tassel

If you want a longer tassel, work the same way, except use a 3½-inch square of cardboard and wrap the thread around about sixty-five times.

Tassel Cap

Any tassel may be trimmed with a crocheted tassel cap. Work as follows:
 Ch 5, sl st to first ch to form ring; ch 2, 15 hdc in ring. Do not sl st to first ch to end, but continue working 1 hdc in each hdc until the cap measures approximately ½ inch. Fasten off. With crochet hook, pull the tie threads of the tassel through the cap and through the ch-5 ring. Pull the cap down evenly over the top of the tassel.

6-15. Thread wound around cardboard.

6-16. Thread pulled through before threads of tassel are cut.

MAKING FRINGES

A fringe consists of loose, hanging threads attached to the work. Fringes can be used as trims for bedspreads, shawls, or other crocheted items. Listed below are several types of fringes suitable for crocheted pieces.

111

Looped-Chain Fringes

If you are attaching fringe onto a crocheted edge, work as follows:

Fasten thread into edge with a sl st. *Ch st twice the desired length of the fringe, sl st back into the same st at the beg, sl st in next 2 sts of edge, rep from * across.

Single-Strand Fringe

To attach fringe onto a crocheted edge fasten thread into edge with a sl st. Sl st in first st of edge. *Ch 16 sts or desired length. Working 2nd ch from hook, work sl sts in each ch back along ch. Sl st in next 2 sts along edge. Rep from * to end.

6-17. Double-Chain Fringe.

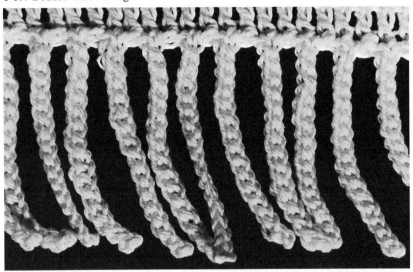

6-18. Single-Chain Fringe.

112

Cut-Thread Fringe

Cut a few lengths of thread, each twice the desired length of fringe. Insert crochet hook into edge of work. Double thread lengths over the hook and pull slightly through the work to form a loop. (See diagram.) Bring ends of thread through the loop and draw up tightly to secure. (See diagram.) Repeat procedure across the edge, placing fringe ⅛ to ½ inch apart.

If you are adding the fringe to crocheted work, start by working a foundation chain row and one row of single crochet. Insert hook through the single crochet and proceed same as above, making a fringe in alternating single crochets.

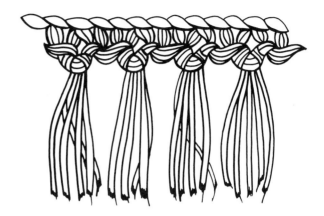

6-19. Cut-Thread Fringe.

6-20. Pulling threads through work.

6-21. Pulling threads through loop.

113

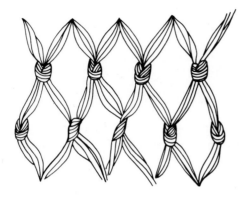

6-22. Latticework Fringe.

Lattice Fringe

A cut-thread fringe may be knotted in an alternating fashion to create latticework. Apply fringe following directions for cut fringe, but using longer threads. Next, take half the threads from each of two neighboring groups and tie in an overhand knot. Repeat across. Add another row of knots alternating them from the first row.

MAKING BRAIDS

Crocheted braids are yet another way to add an interesting touch to your work. (See Figure 6-23.)

Braid #1 (top braid in photograph)

Work as follows:
   Ch 6, sl st to first ch to form ring. Ch 3 (2 dc, 2 tr, 3 dc) in ring. Ch 6, turn. *Make 1 dc between

ch 3 and 1 dc; ch 3, turn, (2 dc, 2 tr, 3 dc) in ch-6 sp; ch 6, turn, rep from * until desired length is achieved. End with (2 dc 2 tr, 3 dc). Work an edging for the braid as follows: *Ch 4, 1 sc, in 1-dc sp of next group, rep from * to end.

Braid #2 (second from top in photograph)

Work as follows:
   Ch to length desired.
ROW 1: Make 1 hdc in 2nd ch from hook and in each remaining ch to end.
ROW 2: Ch 2, turn. Sk 1 hdc (*1 hdc, ch 1, 1 hdc) in next hdc, sk 1 hdc, rep from * across. End with 1 hdc in last hdc.
ROW 3: Ch 2, turn. Make 1 hdc in first sp, *make (1 hdc, ch 2, 1 hdc) in sp between next (1 hdc, ch sp, 1 hdc) sk (1 hdc, ch sp, 1 hdc) rep from * to end. End with 1 hdc in last sp.

Braid #3 (second from bottom in photograph)

Work as follows:
   Ch 6, sl st to form ring. Ch 2, 6 hdc in ring; ch 4, 1 hdc in ring; ch 1, turn. *Make 6 hdc in ch-4 sp just worked, ch 4, 1 hdc in same sp, ch 1, turn; rep from * until desired length is achieved.
   Once the braid has been worked the desired length, work 6 hdc in ch-4 sp just worked, continue with 1 hdc in each of first 4 hdc of next 6-hdc group, **ch 4, sk 3 hdc in next 6-hdc group, 1 sc in next hdc, rep from ** to corner end of braid.
   Work around corner as follows: Ch 4, 1 sc in each of 4 hdc of next set of 6 hdc around corner; 1 hdc in each of next 2 hdc, 2 hdc in beg of ch-6 ring, 1 hdc in next ch-4 sp, 1 hdc in each of next 4 hdc, *** ch 4, sk 3 hdc of next 6-hdc group, 1 sc in next hdc, repeat from *** to end. End with ch 4, sl st to 1st group of 6 hdc. Fasten off.

114

6-23. From top to bottom: Braids #1 through #4.

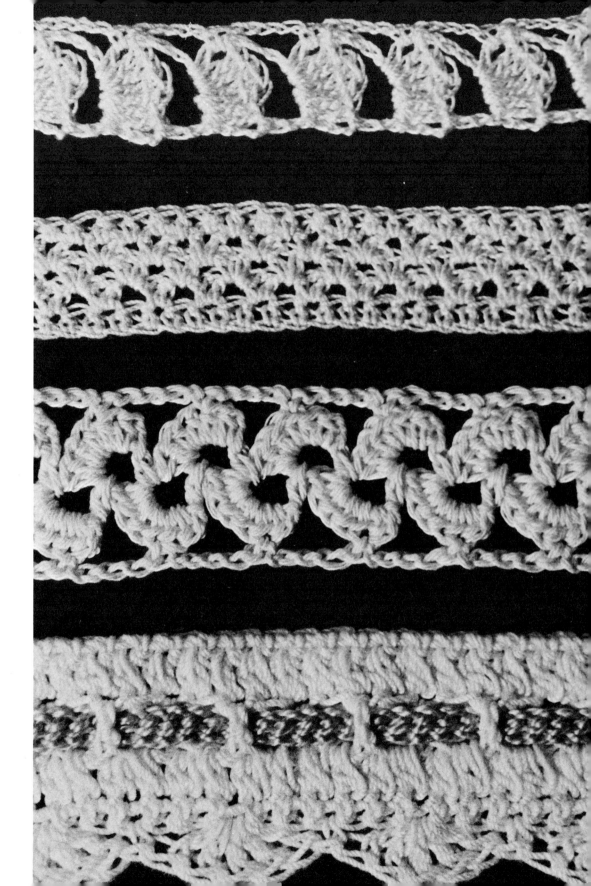

Braid #4

Work as follows:

TO START: Ch to the desired length.

ROW 1: Make 1 sc in first ch from hook and continue with 1 sc in each ch across.

ROW 2: Ch 3, turn. In first sc, crochet 1 cluster as follows: (Yo hook, insert hook in sc, yo hook, pull yarn through, yo hook, insert in same sc, pull up, yo hook and pull through all lps on hook.) Work 1 cluster in each sc to end.

ROW 3: Ch 4, turn. Sk 1 cluster and 1 dc in next cluster, * ch 1, 1 dc in next cluster, rep from * until end.

ROW 4: Ch 3, turn. Make 1 cluster in base of ch 3, * 1 cluster in ch-1 sp, 1 cluster in next dc, rep from * across.

ROW 5: Ch 1, turn. Work 1 sc in each st across.

ROW 6: Ch 3, turn. Make 2 dc in base of ch 3, * sk 1 sc, 1 sc in next sc, sk 2 sc, 5 dc in next sc [1 shell made], rep from * across.

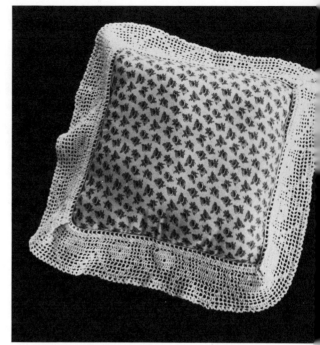

6-24. Pillow With Filet-Lace Trim.

PILLOW WITH FILET-LACE TRIM

Materials

1 ball (200 yards) mercerized crochet cotton, number 10
pillow
sewing thread to match
sewing needle

Hook

size 3

Gauge

8 dc = 1 inch
4 rows = 1 inch

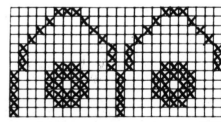

6-25. Graph for filet border.   START

Directions

Study Figures 6-24 and 6-25 and read the directions in Chapter 3 for filet crochet.

Filet-Lace Trim

TO START: Ch 370 or desired length to reach around pillow edges.

116

ROW 1: In 4th ch from hook, * work 1 dc, sk next ch, ch 1, rep from * to end of ch. Turn work.

ROW 2: Work 1 dc in first dc, * in ch-1 sp, work 2 dc, 1 dc in next dc, in next ch-1 sp work 1 dc, rep from * across. Turn work.

ROW 3: Work 1 sc in each dc across. Turn work.

ROW 4 – 14: Follow graph, repeating motif across entire row. Use dc for each st.

ROW 15 (edging): Make 1 sc into next dc, * ch 3, 1 sc into next dc, rep from * around. Fasten off.

NOTE: Sk dc of filled-in sps. Starch work lightly and block.

Assembly

With tiny whip stitches sew the lace to pillow edge. Overlap corners of lace to pillow corners. Sc ends tog at 1 corner.

HANKIE WITH LACE TRIM

Materials

1 ball (250 yards) mercerized crochet cotton, number 30, or tatting thread
Irish linen handkerchief

Hook

size 10

Gauge

5 rows = 1 inch

Directions

Study Figure 6-26.

TO START: Work a sc base around all 4 sides of handkerchief. Work 2 sc in each corner space. End with a sl st to first sc.

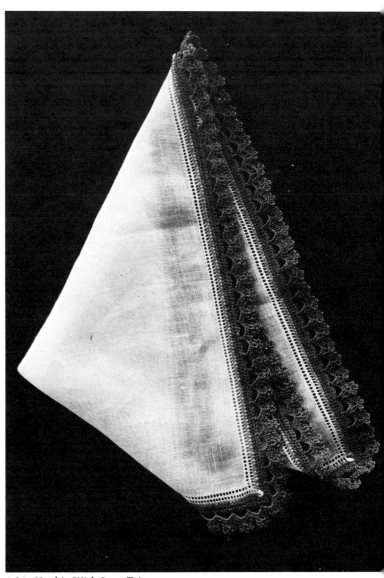

6-26. Hankie With Lace Trim.

117

ROW 1: * Make (1 sc, 4 dc, 1 sc) in each of next 6 sc, rep from * around 4 sides of hankie. This will give a scallop effect. Work corners as follows: (1 sc, 4 dc, 1 sc) in each sc of corner sp. End with sl st to first sc.

ROW 2: * Ch 5, 1 sc in next sc, rep from * around 4 sides of hankie. End with sl st to first sc.

ROW 3: * Make (4 hdc, ch 4, 4 hdc) in each ch-5 sp, rep from * in remaining ch-5 sps around hankie.

ROW 4: Sl st up 4 hdc to ch-4 sp; (ch 4, 1 sc, ch 4, 1 sc, ch 4, 1 sc) in ch-4 sp; * ch 2, 1 sc between ch-4 sp from previous row, ch 2 (1 sc, ch 4, 1 sc, ch 4, 1 sc, ch 4, 1 sc) in next ch-4 sp, rep from * around hankie. Fasten off.

COLLAR WITH LACE TRIM

Materials

1 ball (450 yards) mercerized crochet cotton, number 20
sewing thread to match
sewing needle

Hook

size 10

Gauge

7 rows = 1 inch

Directions

Study Figure 6-27.

TO START: Ch 6, sl st to first ch to form ring.

ROW 1: Ch 6, 1 sc in ring, * ch 6, turn, 1 sc in newly formed ring, rep from * until desired length is achieved for collar to be trimmed.

ROW 2 (top of lace): Make 5 dc in first ch-6 sp, *5 dc in next ch-6 sp, rep from * to end. Continue around and crochet 5 dc on other side in ch-6 sps. End with sl st to first dc.

ROW 3: Make 1 hdc in first dc and in each dc [5 in all], * ch 4, 1 hdc in next 5 dc, rep from * to end. Sl st to first hdc.

ROW 4: Ch 7, turn. Make 1 sc in ch-4 sp, * ch 7, 1 sc in next ch-4 sp, rep from * to end.

ROW 5: Ch 1, turn. Make 10 sc in each ch-7 sp. (This can be done in a contrasting color.)

ROW 6: St st along edge up to next group of sc, ch 4, * 1 sc in 3rd sc of next group, ch 4, rep from * to end. Fasten off.

To attach lace to collar: Any blouse you have which has a collar can be made just a little lovelier with the addition of handmade crochet lace. The collar lace is attached to the collar with hand sewing. This gives neatness to the work and also control which a sewing machine does not give. Use tiny whip stitches so that they are not noticeable to the eye. If there are points on your collar, gently turn the lace and work it around the point. After the lace is completely attached to the collar, steam press it on low heat. Your lace will last a long time if hand-laundered with mild detergent in warm water. Rinse thoroughly and allow to drip dry. Touch up with a steam-pressing.

6-27. Collar With Lace Trim.

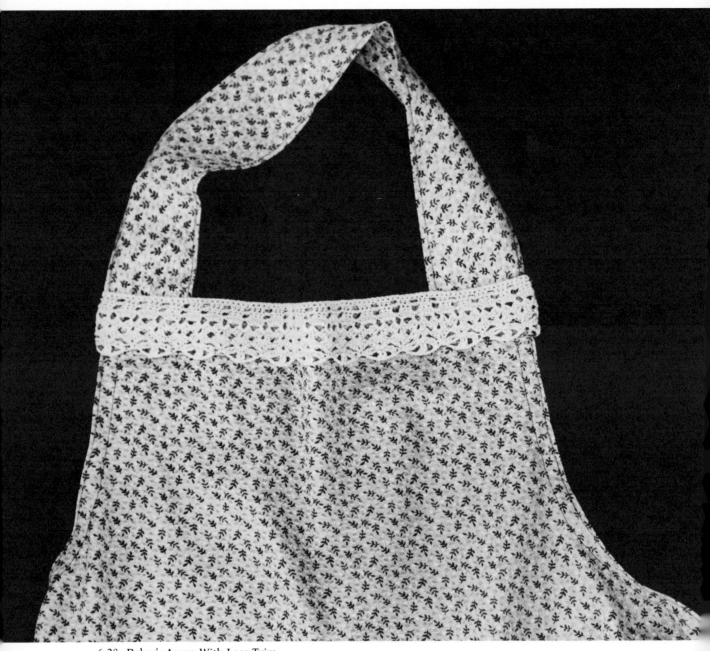

6-28. Baker's Apron With Lace Trim.

BAKER'S APRON WITH TRIM

Materials

1 ball (200 yards) mercerized crochet cotton, number 10
baker's apron or 2 yards cotton or cotton blend fabric, 44/45 inches wide to make your own
sewing thread to match
sewing needle

Gauge

6 rows = 1 inch

Directions

Study Figures 6-28 and 6-29.
TO START: Make a ch 12½ inches in length.
ROW 1: Make 1 sc in 2nd ch from hook, 1 sc in each ch to end. End with ch 2, turn.
ROW 2: Make 1 dc in each of next 2 sc, * ch 3, sk 1 sc, 1 dc in each of next 3 sc, rep from * to end. End with ch 3, turn.
ROW 3: Make 1 hdc in each of next 2 dc, * ch 2, 1 hdc in each of next 3 dc, rep from * to end. End with ch 3, turn.
ROW 4: Make 1 dc in each of next 2 hdc, (3 dc, ch 1, 3 dc) in next ch-2 sp, rep from * to end. End with 1 dc in each of next 3 hdc, ch 3, turn.
ROW 5: Make 1 dc in each of next 3 dc, (3 dc, ch 1, 3 dc) in ch-1 sp, rep from * to end. End with 1 dc in each of next 3 dc, ch 3, turn.
ROW 6: *(2 tr tr, ch 3, 2 tr tr) in ch-1 sp, ch 1, 1 sc in next ch-1 sp, ch 1, rep from * to end. End with ch 3, sl st to top of ch 3. Fasten off. Steam press with medium heat.

6-29. Detail of lace trim.

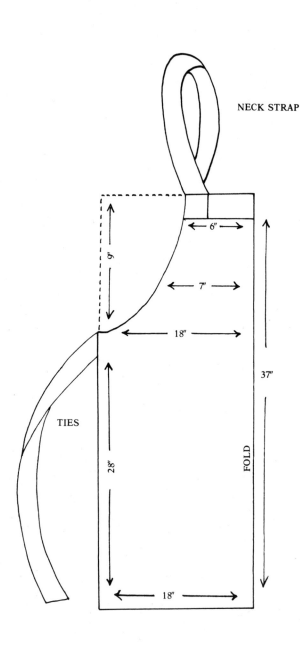

NECK STRAP

6"

9'

7"

18"

37"

TIES

28"

FOLD

18"

6-30. Pattern for baker's apron.

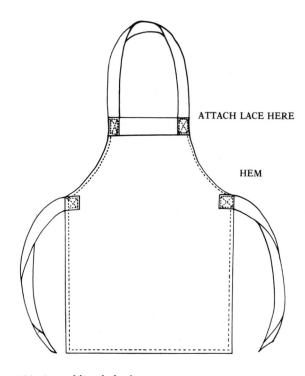

ATTACH LACE HERE

HEM

6-31. Assembling baker's apron.

To make your own apron: Cut an apron pattern from newspaper, tissue paper, or brown wrapping paper. [See diagram.] Use a dark felt-tipped pen for marking the outline. Pin pattern to fabric, placing fold of pattern on fold of fabric. Cut pattern out from fabric. Also cut 1 neck strap, 5½ inches wide by 21 inches long and 2 ties, each 3½ inches wide by 40 inches long. Sew neck strap by folding fabric in half lengthwise with right sides together. Stitch a seam along the edge ⅝ inch. Leave ends open.

Turn right side out and press. Sew the ties, using the same procedure as for the strap, but sewing 1 end shut on each tie and leaving 1 end open. Machine-stitch a narrow ½-inch hem around the entire edge of apron. Fold ends of neck strap and ties up 1½ inches and pin to apron. (See diagram.) Topstitch these ends to apron and machine- or hand-stitch lace to top of apron. Press entire apron.

To attach edging to apron: Machine- or hand-stitch lace to top of apron with whip stitches.

HEARTS AND FLOWERS PILLOWCASE FILET TRIM

Materials

2 balls (200 yards each) mercerized crochet cotton, number 10
2 pillowcases or 2 yards of fabric, 44/45 inch wide to make your own
sewing thread to match
sewing needle

6-32. Hearts and Flowers Pillowcase Filet Trim.

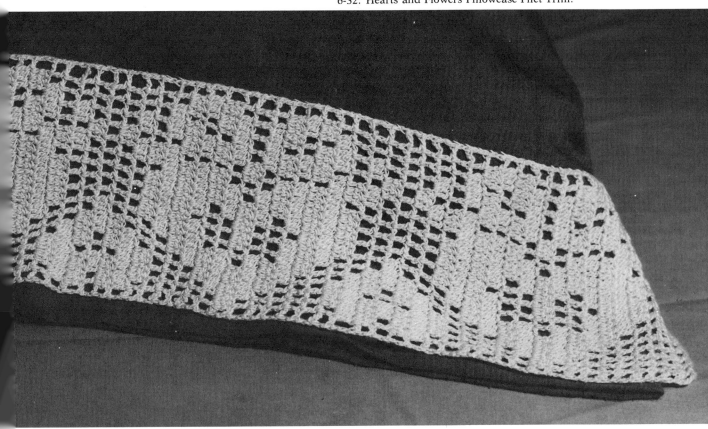

Hook

size 7

Gauge

10 dc = 1 inch

Directions

Study Figure 6-32.

TO START: Ch 40. Dc in 6th ch from hook, * ch 1, sk 1 ch, and dc in next. Rep from * until the end of the ch. Continue row by row following the graph. The filled-in sps are done in double mesh crochet. [Read page 54 for directions on double mesh crochet.] The sps are worked in dc. Be sure to keep the sides of lace even and ending squares also. This can be accomplished by always chaining 6 to turn and ending the rows with a dc in 3rd ch of ch 6. Rep pat of hearts and ribbons to the desired length.

TO FINISH: Block the pieces. (Read instructions at the beg of Chapter 3 on how to block.) Sew lace onto pillowcases with very small overcast stitches. Patience is necessary. The hand sewing gives a nicer look than machine sewing; it doesn't bunch and has a nice flat look.

To make your own pillowcases: Cut patterns to fit your bed pillows plus allowing enough on the ends to cover. Hem ends of cases the same width as lace plus ½ inch. Proceed to sew lace on cases after blocking. Press pillowcases thoroughly.

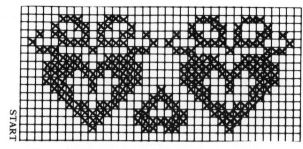

6-33. Graph for Hearts and Flowers.

124

BIBLIOGRAPHY

Books

Blackwell, Liz. *A Treasury of Crochet Patterns.* New York: Charles Scribner's Sons, 1979.

Filet Crochet from Priscilla Books of 1926. New York: Dover Publications, 1979.

Mon Tricot—250 Stitches and Patterns to Knit and Crochet. West Caldwell, New Jersey: Curtis Circulation Company, 21 Henderson Drive.

Orr, Anne. *Crochet Designs of Anne Orr.* New York: Dover Publications, 1978.

Ray, Juliana and Bokoli, Madeline. *Crochet Designs from Hungary.* New York: Dover Publications, 1973.

Ryan, Mildred Graves. *The Complete Encyclopedia of Stitchery.* New York: Nelson Doubleday Co., 1979.

Sibmacher, Johan. *Baroque Charted Designs for Needlework.* New York: Dover Publications, 1975.

Magazines

Filet Crochet Patterns
Box 337 AO
Seabrook, NH 03874

Crochet World
Box 337 AO
Seabrook, NH 03874

Magic Crochet Magazine
Publishers Service
4 Neil Drive
Old Bethpage, NY 11804

Old Time Crochet Patterns and Designs
Box 337 OA
Seabrook, NH 03874

METRIC CONVERSION CHART

Linear Measure

1 inch = 2.54 centimeters
12 inches = 1 foot = 0.3048 meter
3 feet = 1 yard = 0.9144 meter

Square Measure

1 square inch = 6.452 square centimeters
144 square inches = 1 square foot = 929.03 square centimeters
9 square feet = 1 square yard = 0.8362 square meter

126

INDEX